Rapportselling Tales

Successful Selling Strategies for Engaging Customers

Paul Archer

High House Publishing

First published in Great Britain in 2012 by High House Publishing, High House, Priors Norton, Gloucestershire, GL2 9LS, United Kingdom

Printed and bound in Great Britain by Lulu.com

Edited by Lynnette Carter

Cover designed by Felicia Cornish

ISBN 978-0-9571738-0-4 (Paperback)

ISBN 978-0-9571738-1-1 (eBook)

For all your sales training needs, in house requirements contact Paul at

www.archertraining.com

www.paularcher.com

paul@paularcher.com

+44 (0)1452 730276

This book is dedicated to my family and close friends, for their inspiration and support.

And especially to my dad and late mum, Denis and Ilse, for the love and guidance they have given to me over the years and continue to do so.

TABLE OF CONTENTS

Chapter 1 – Looking back

In which we first meet Doug, hugely successful and looking back on his career

New Year's Eve 2035

I love Christmas. There's something about this festive holiday that everyone seems to enjoy. Whatever your age, place in society, colour, race or creed...everyone enjoys the break.

For me, it's especially exciting as my eldest son has just been accepted into University, although a little late. He went travelling after his exams with Australia as his destination, but got caught up in the awful teleportation saga that rocked the nation throughout the autumn. Neal was so keen to use this new invention and it seemed the ideal opportunity to get across the other side of the world in a micro-second. But he didn't reckon it taking over 4 months.

"Caught in a space time continuum," they said. Pretty frightening for my wife and I, but at least we could talk to him during those terrible months. He's now safe and sound, although rather shaken.

So here we are, New Year 2035, scorning the modern inventions which I still believe were never thoroughly tested. Enough of that. At least, Neal is fine, fit and healthy and starts University early in January.

I must say, I do feel proud of my children. In fact, I might go as far as to say that I'm pretty pleased with the way the family has evolved over the last 20 years of marriage to my gorgeous wife. Three beautiful children, all grown up now. Still a big financial burden on me, but I love that.

Do indulge me and allow me to explain who I am and why I'm here. My name is Douglas Ballantyne. My friends call me Doug... and you can, too. It's New Years' Eve 2035. But I already told you that, didn't I? Must stop using too many *yes* tags. Everyone's out tonight. My wife is out working and the children are partying somewhere, but I mustn't call them children anymore. Neal is 19 and the other two are 17 and 16. My wife's a midwife and a very good one, too. She loves the job, trained for it later in life and really excels in it. She's always been good with people and finds this skill so useful when dealing with her clients. Fancy term, that -- clients, but I guess it's appropriate.

She has a knack of making anyone feel relaxed, which is a must for someone about to give birth. I thought I'd wait up to see the New Year in and see in the fireworks, which always look spectacular from the back garden. I've a glass of my favourite tipple – French brandy from the banks of the Charente – lovely. The bottle very close by and the fire is glowing in the corner of the living room. I think another log maybe, so where's the remote control? I must say these house robots have really advanced in the last few years, so I treated myself at Christmas. Voice controlled they are, but the remote control device works just as good. That's done, excellent.

I'm a lucky man. Wonderful family, wouldn't want for much really, successful career so far, with at least 25 working years to go, since the government extended the retirement age to 75. But I don't mind as I really enjoy what I do and couldn't see myself not working. Would bore me senseless.

All evening, I've been contemplating my career in this business and churning around in my mind exactly what I've achieved, the mistakes I've made, the lucky breaks I've had, the events I've experienced. It's such a lot that I've decided to share it with you.

I'm the Sales and Marketing Director for a large financial services company and my team sells financial products to customers all over the country. Our customers look for all of their financial worries to be taken care of and look to trust my advisers in every way possible. At last count, we had 450 advisers scattered around the UK, but I have a strong management team who looks after their every whim and request.

It's taken me 20 years to get there though, and it hasn't been easy. I started right down at the foot of the ladder in the New Year of 2010. Ah... I can see myself now -- fresh, excited and raring to go in my new job. Boy, I looked young then, too. Let's go back to the great recession of 2010.

Chapter 2 – Getting motivated to learn

In which Doug realises he has a ton of work to do and finally discovers the secret to motivation

New Year 2010.

I looked out the window and could see the brightness of the morning shimmering across the city rooftops. It was just after 9 in the morning and I was feeling decidedly rough I can tell you. My neighbour's surprise party was a fabulous event. Londoners always know how to enjoy a party and let their hair down, and Reg next door didn't blow this reputation. A brilliant night, but now, a startling hangover.

Today is to be spent recuperating, but also revising my pre-course work before next week's residential training course in Hartford.

Let me fill you in further. On leaving college, I've had all sorts of jobs but always connected with people. My last job was very relevant in the current recession; I worked as a New Claims Adviser at the Jobcentre Plus. Really interesting to interview people who wanted to sign on and get a new job. Rather stressful, too. Also rewarding, but at age 30 I couldn't see myself working at the Jobcentre for the rest of my career so I looked for a complete new direction.

New Year 2010

What about me. I'm 30, but I've already told you that. I'm very single. My last serious girlfriend was Heidi, who left me for a professional life guard two years ago. I wouldn't have minded except we were on holiday together in Biarritz, South of France and she met Alain whilst I was in bed with French tummy troubles. Too many mussels one evening, which didn't agree with me. Alain was our surfing tutor and also a Surveillant de Baignade – that's a life guard to you and I.

We departed on amicable grounds, mind you, and sold our flat at the top of the housing market and made a handsome profit so it wasn't all that bad. Ever since then, I've been renting here in London and being very single and enjoying every moment.

Don't get me wrong. I do want to settle down and have children, but I haven't met the right person since my heart was shattered during the summer of 2007.

So my attentions turn to my career direction. It came in the form of a Financial Adviser. Never did this before, although always have been interested in money -- making it that is. Seriously though, I've always been fascinated in how people can borrow money, take out credit cards, have life assurance, car insurance, invest in pensions, save in ISAs...the list goes on. So I took the plunge and applied for the job based here in North London. After a rigorous interview process, I landed the job and start my training course next Monday at the company's head office in Hartford. Officially I've been employed by the chain since the second week in December, but I've been working in the local offices doing my pre-course studying.

It's a chain of estate agents with around 250 branches across the South, South West and London. A little worrying because they haven't sold many houses of late as the housing market has been in the doldrums, but things are picking up nicely, especially here in North London. My main role will be to help clients of the agents with their mortgages and re-mortgages, but the Area Manager is keen for us to develop our own clients and give them advice on all their financial needs, which is life assurance, health insurance, loans, investments.

And that's where the training comes in. There's a lot to do, which is one of the main reasons I accepted the job. I haven't learned anything new since leaving Sixth Form 11 years' ago, so it would be good to get the brain in action again.

I'm a little nervous about the job, but the Area Manager assured me I'd be brilliant at it and could earn a lot of money. Nice that she had confidence in me. Besides, my experience in interviewing and speaking with people would hold me in good stead.

Apparently they are 10 of us who began at the same time. That's really good because we can help each other and bounce ideas, as well. We've already met, so to speak, during the online meetings. Let me explain.

The studying has been good. Hard work, mind you, but with the internet, they have made it interesting. I've got various exams to take and plenty of studying to do. All I have to do is log on using my laptop and the company sends me the learning material via the web. There are videos to watch, podcasts and reading material, activities, and case studies, which are designed to get me thinking about giving customers advice.

Lots of tests, as well, to keep me on the edge and every couple of days we all log on and meet up online. This part is really cool. The laptop has a built-in webcam so we can all see each other. Our trainer is there, as well, and we can talk and ask questions, after which she explains things areas in which we are stuck. I must admit, though, to looking forward to the real courses that start next Monday. It's great seeing people on the internet and instant messaging them, but I do miss the real life stuff -- you know, actually meeting someone and listening to people, watching them, sharing ideas. I'm really looking forward to that part, and also, meeting Vicky from Southampton. She looks really chilled.

Enough of that. Let's focus. I must say that is a bit of a challenge at the moment. Focussing, that is, with the studies. The problem I find is that much of it is quite lonely. I'm having to struggle on my own and keep myself motivated. What's more, they tell me that once I'm up and running as a financial adviser in the offices, I'm pretty much on my own and I need to just get on and succeed.

This does worry me a little. After all, most of my previous jobs weren't in selling and I didn't have this kind of pressure to cope with. I also had a team of people around me to keep me motivated and bosses on my tail if I slipped up in any way. Although I won't miss that, I do need to learn how to be more self motivated and driven.

Particularly now as I've got some really hard and complex studying to do so I can pass these exams. Where's that laptop? Must get on. What was that? Ah, saved by the mobile.

"Hiya Jeff, how's it going?"

"Hey, Doug, how's the hangover?"

"Terrible, but I'll be fine. What's up, Jeff?"

As always, a man gets to the point on the phone with not a huge amount of small talk. Jeff and I had been best pals for three years now. We met at the Jobcentre Plus. We were both New Claims Advisers and seemed to have plenty in common. Jeff is the same age as me, totally single and such a party animal. As soon as he walks into the room, he lights the whole place up, he just has that sparky personality and attracts masses of people towards him, especially the girls. He's a good mate to have.

He's got his own place near the park, a swanky pad, too. Not sure where he got the money to buy it on his wages. I think he has some very rich parents -- lucky chap. We get on brilliantly and promised each other that we would be each other's Best Man at our weddings, although, I can't see Jeff ever getting hitched.

"We're having a little gathering over here to celebrate New Year's Day around 2 o'clock. Got the guys coming over from the Jobcentre and the girls from Dalston office are coming over too. Fancy it?"

"Sure do. See you later, Jeff. Thanks for phoning."

That's a shame. Have to put the studying on hold for the day, but after all, it is a Bank Holiday; no one else is working. Besides, I've got the weekend to catch up with the studies.

The alarm clock shouted at me around 8 o'clock, and I staggered downstairs. Eating my Golden Grahams, I glanced at the laptop in the corner. Poor thing hadn't had any attention for almost a week as I managed to do some studying on Monday afternoon. I was becoming a little nervous that I was falling behind and wouldn't be prepared for this Monday morning when the course started. At least I'd have all of Sunday because Hartford was only a short journey for me on Monday morning. All the others were staying overnight in the hotel.

My mobile sang out a text message. It was from Jeff. Wanted to know if I had a good time last night. What was I doing today?

So I typed in a return message.

"Studying c u nxt wk."

A strong coffee later and I opened my laptop. It was company issued – a Dell and excellent spec as well -- built in webcam, fast, good sized screen and a dongle to access the internet at fast speeds from anywhere. And they foot the mobile phone bill, as well. Really good bit of kit.

Let's check out Facebook Chat first, see who's around…

No, you must get on, Doug. So I opened up the day's lesson -- in fact, it was last Tuesday's lesson. I was that far behind. And in the queue was a further four lessons. I calculated that each lesson takes around 1½ hours, so including today's…that's almost 8 hours.

I can do that, no problem…23 people online on Facebook, there's my brother in Chicago…best to wish him a Happy New Year…Google +, let's see who's online…

This is useless. Must get into my studying, but first let's say 'hi' to my bro.

"Hi Bro, you chatting?"

Always a delay when on Facebook when the other person decides to drop who they're talking to or chat to you.

"Howdy Doug. How's it going back there in The Smoke?"

"Going well, Steve thanks. How's the Windy City?"

My brother Steve had moved out with his firm 9 months ago and was having a whale of a time. Flat paid for by his firm, great salary and an Englishman in Chicago. His life seemed pretty rosy.

"Windy City is fine. Very, very cold. How's the new job?"

"Good. Lots of training and I'm behind. Too much going out with Jeff and the guys."

"Is Jeff causing probs?

"No, he's OK, just can't get into it at moment."

"Need some motivation then Doug?"

"I do, actually. Can I get some from the chemist?"

"Lol."

"Seriously Bro, I need some motivation. Any ideas?"

"Yes, Doug, I do. Stumbled across this resource on the net, the Motivation Queen, Illinois."

"Thanks Bro, have a great time. Gotta dash."

What a website. Wow, she's some maven of sales motivation. She's a speaker, trainer, coach, author...what else can she do? Ah, I see a products page saying downloads available immediately. First I must sign up for her weekly motivation tip newsletter. There. That's done now. I download her podcasts on motivation that might give me some answers.

An hour later, $39 poorer, iPod loaded, I lay on my bed, closed my eyes and began to listen to the Queen.

> "A number of years ago, Imran Khan, the acclaimed captain of the Pakistan cricket team was being accused by a press reporter as being arrogant. He replied that he'd always imagined being in the Pakistan cricket team so the goal of being captain was never too high a goal to achieve.
>
> Have you ever wondered why some people are just so dedicated, focussed and successful in what they do? The simple answer is that these people set goals. Channel energy to a single point and you can have immense power. Take a torch light and make the light as fine and precise as possible and you get a laser able to cut through metal. You're on your two week vacation tomorrow and you need to clear your desk and outstanding email and calls by the end of the day...and you miraculously do it. That's the power of setting goals.
>
> Take a human being. Yes, we can bumble along happily for years and I know many people that do this not getting anywhere in particular, but are quite happy doing so. But if you want to achieve things in your life – reach your potential, have a happy retirement or whatever it is that you want... the simple truth is you need defined and written goals in all aspects of your life.

I'm going to tell you about six strategies to help you set your goals and get what you want out of your life."

As I listened to the Queen, a bolt of lightning shuddered through me. I suddenly realised where I was going wrong. Why did I want this new job? Where was my life going? I was lured in at the interview with the promise of earning a decent wage plus unlimited commissions and bonus. That's not enough – I need to set my goals and this will motivate me to get on with the studying. Let's get back to the Queen as she's got six things for me.

"First, get a strategy to do your goals and stick to it.

You need a definition of what is ultimate success for you. This can be way off into the horizon and it doesn't matter whether you just want to retire happily in a little cottage by the sea or retire a millionaire. Your ultimate aim in life is personal. You may not see your life that far ahead and again, that doesn't matter since it's your life.

Now comes the clever part. Next, write down your long term goals which are your visions or strategy, which can be 10 years plus. Next the medium term goals, i.e. about 3 to 5 years, which is the planning to get to the long term goals. Then your short term goals which should be yearly, and again, these should feed into the medium term goals. Short term goals can be 'to dos'.

With your short term or annual goals, I would further break these down into quarters. Q1 (January, February and March), Q2 (April, May, June), Q3 and Q4. Then take the three month quarter to achieve them. If you don't achieve any just carry it forward.

Sounds easy. Well done Queen. Let me pause you for a moment. Right. What is it that I want? Do you know I've never really sat down to think it through? Let's dream a little. In 20 years' time when I'm 50, I'd like to be working for myself, wealthy, happy, with a lovely home in the country. Kids? Yes. Dog? Absolutely. I want all those things. I'd like to be good at my job and control big budgets and large teams.

In 10 years' time, I'd like to have a young family and be very settled. In fact, I'd like this in the next 5 years. Work-wise, I can see myself being very successful as a Financial Adviser in 5 years' time, earning good money, owning my own house with my young family. Actually, this is an important part for me, a nice house. How about a company car as well? No, I'd like one of these in a years' time. A cool BMW, always wanted one of those.

What about short term? How long did the Queen say these should be? Yearly, I think. In a year from now, I need to be achieving my targets, seeing lots of clients, doing well, having loads of friends in the Agency. I'd like to have all my exams under my belt and be looked up to by my fellow Financial Advisers.

In six months... definitely have all my exams out of the way and be settled in the Stoke Newington Branch. What did they call it? That's right -- Competent Adviser Status. All my training out of the way and writing a minimum number of business cases.

Cricky, 6 months isn't far away really. What about my quarterly goals? Studies, exams, courses, learning the ropes. That's it; I've got to get cracking on these now. Wow. Thanks, Queen. OK, let's hear what else you have to say.

"Let me give you my second strategy now, called Pareto's Law. Sounds like some new Attorney drama on NBC. I'm sure we've all heard of Pareto, the Italian economist, who devised a law that rings truth everywhere you go. Pareto's Law, when planning your goals, says that we get 80% of our results from 20% of our goals. Prioritise them and don't have too many. So with all those fabulous goals you've set yourself, prioritise them.

My next strategy is to carry out a SWOT, at least annually. SWOT stands for your Strengths, Weaknesses, Opportunities and Threats. Brainstorm these, then set learning goals to maximise your strengths, minimise your weaknesses, eliminate threats and optimise your opportunities. Look ahead and futurise what might happen. In my business in 15 years time we will have holograms of sales speakers and motivational trainers teaching things to people as the cost of travel will be prohibitive except for only the most important journeys. Sending my hologram across the world will be cheap, instantaneous and virtually the same as my being there. After all -- I will be. Spooky stuff, but it will happen and I need to be able to keep my own learning up to speed to deal with this before it happens and puts me out of business. Change. Knowledge and skills can help you do this.

Here's my favourite strategy. Phrase your goal in a positive sense. This is really important, particularly if you are a "towards" person in achieving goals. The "towards" strategy has been proven to be more robust when setting goals. Aim towards something rather than away from something. For example rather than losing 12 lbs, think about gaining a better shape and being able to fit into those trousers.

When we write our goals in a negative sense, such as 'Don't work on later than 5pm every day,' a strange thing happens. The brain will focus on the *don't* and get a little confused, so it processes working on after 5pm before it can commute the word 'don't'. The net result? The brain will think it needs to work beyond 5pm before it can stop.

My second to last strategy for you, now. Stretch yourself. Stretch yourself when writing your goals. Just enough to make it a challenge, but don't stretch too far – that's when we pull our backs. Seriously though, you'd be amazed what humans are capable of when we set out minds to it.

For my 40th birthday, my husband bought for me a three hour excursion with a Police Traffic Officer in his excessively fast Buick. Was I excited? The first lesson was how to control a car whilst skidding, then he taught us how to drive really fast. The finale of the lesson was to take the wheel of his hideously fast patrol car and drive as fast as I could along a public Freeway. I tell you, I was scared.

A friend of mine came along to keep me company and this was great as we could make mistakes together and not feel so bad. But to make a mistake when driving at more than 100mph on a Freeway could be dangerous. Very dangerous. 'You take the wheel first,' said the traffic cop 'and take us as fast as you can, but don't forget what I taught you'.

But I know a little bit about setting goals so I told myself that I would exceed 115mph. I knew my limits!

Off I went cruising at 70mph. 'OK,' said the cop, 'Let's take it up'. And off I went 80... 90... 100mph... 110... 118mph. Was I thrilled. Safe and relieved, I slowed down and let my friend, Diane, have a go.

Within a minute she was doing 136mph. I asked her afterwards how she managed it. Diane said that after I'd gone first and she could see herself going faster than me, it was easier.

So stretch your goals – you'll be amazed as to what we are capable of doing. 13 years ago, David Beckham of LA Galaxy fame, was the only real master free-kick taker in the English Premiership. He was so good they named a film after him, *Bend it like Beckham*. Nowadays every team has one or two specialist free-kick takers.

After Roger Bannister had broken the 4 minute mile in May 1956, after years of training and dedication, within the same year, another 37 people had done so. And the following year a whopping 300 people achieved the 4 minute mile.

So stretch your goals just that little bit more. Instead of focussing around 115mph, I should have targeted myself for 130. Just that little bit faster."

Phew! Queen, these are great strategies. Let me summarise. I've got to prioritise them with Pareto, talk about what I want rather than what I don't want, do a SWOT on my skills and stretch myself. OK Queen, in 20 years' time I want to be the boss of this company and run the whole Financial Services Division and in 10 years' time I want to be the Area Director. That'll show 'em. Last few minutes of the Queen now.

"My last strategy for you folks is to measure your goal; we're supposed to put measures on our goals. Many people talk about SMART goals where the M stands for measurable. But some big goals or long term goals are difficult to measure and, quite frankly, this doesn't make them too exciting.

With a really big important goal, instead of a measure, privately create a vision of achieving success with your goal. What will you see, hear and feel when you are triumphant? Who's around you, what's the weather like, what noise is happening, what are you doing? Imagine the scene as vividly as you can. This way you'll know when you've achieved it.

Sometimes it's good to imagine this so clearly in the future. Put a date on it and place this vision on that date in the future. Do all this in your head and, sure enough, you will find a way to achieve this goal.

I first did this in 1995. As a busy corporate sales trainer for a large Pharmaceutical company, I visualised and placed into the future my goal. If this goal was successful, I would be sitting at my office at home with my feet up on the table opening an envelope with a cheque inside from a client who was paying me for some training I had done. I had become my own master. Sure enough, 5 years' later I was there. In my Home office opening a big cheque from a client.

Right now, I want you to take your imagination, and float this into a time in the future and drop down to the *you* in the future time. See yourself achieving the goal you've set. Vividly describe what you see around you, what you can hear, the sounds, the feelings. Associate yourself with the dream and imagine yourself as being there. Now come back from that time, but keep that future vision clearly in your head and return to it time and time again. Good luck, all. This is the Motivation Queen signing off."

Thanks Queen. OK, let's drift now. Come out of my mind, onto the future track to the year 2030. Here I go....and I'm going to plop down into the year 2030 and imagine myself sitting in an armchair hugely successful and happy, the boss of the whole outfit, pulling all the strings, kids, wife, big house in the country....Uhmmm it feels good.

Our training department recommended I keep a learning diary, which I thought was a great idea. I quickly noted down the Queen's 6 strategies to help me remember her top tips.

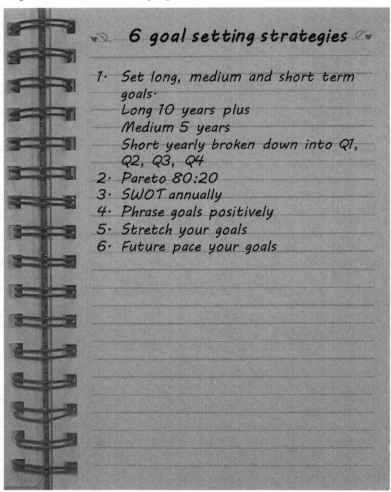

6 goal setting strategies

1. Set long, medium and short term goals.
   Long 10 years plus
   Medium 5 years
   Short yearly broken down into Q1, Q2, Q3, Q4
2. Pareto 80:20
3. SWOT annually
4. Phrase goals positively
5. Stretch your goals
6. Future pace your goals

And sure enough, by Sunday night I'd finished all my studying, was bang up to date, brimming with confidence and getting an early night before tomorrow's big day when the course starts.

Chapter 3 – No one to see

In which Doug realises that sales in the real world is tough and discovers how to get new customers

Vicky was as cute for real as she was on the webcam, but the computer didn't do her personality justice. She reminded me of my friend Jeff, as she could also light up a room just by stepping into it. But she was engaged to a sailor, so any thoughts in that direction had to be quickly quashed.

The training is now over for the time being. I've still a few exams to do, but the main ones are done now. Passed easily, but it was tough. The thing that pulled me together was my vision in my head, which the Motivation Queen helped me create. It kept driving me forward as I so want to achieve my goals. I've also set my first quarter goals now that I'm sitting down in the Estate Agents in Stoke Newington.

This morning I met with Chloe, my Area Manager. Chloe is very experienced and started out by doing my job back in the mid-1990's, so she's got almost 20 years' behind her in this business. She has great respect from everyone in the office; she's very fair, but tough. Doesn't suffer fools gladly, so I'd better keep my nose clean and my figures on the up.

Chloe is married; her husband is also in the business as an Independent Financial Adviser running his own firm. She's got to be in her very early 40's I'd say, but to be honest, no one knows her age. Always immaculately dressed, she oozes confidence and charm. Very professional and very good at her job. I definitely rate her as a sales manager; perhaps, she could become my role-model to look up to, so to reach my goals.

She covers the whole of North London, so has a large area to patrol, but is able to give me a fair bit of her time over the first few months. She says that her main aim is to see me fully signed off in 6 weeks.

Sounds fun.

To be signed off I need to demonstrate that I can do the job to her standard and she needs to see me do it, as well. But that's the problem that I see. We're just not very busy in the office at the moment. We should be. After all, it's springtime in London and the housing market should be booming with first-time buyers flocking to view our desirable residences on our books. We're only just coming out of the Great Credit Crunch, and the supply of mortgages has never been better. I've got some great deals available to me at the moment and some high percentage lending as well.

When I went for the job, they told me that there would be lots of people to speak with and give advice to regarding their financial circumstances. So, working towards my exams and becoming qualified would be the most important hurdle. I overcame that one and passed my exams, but this seems a mightier barrier to me.

I think I'll raise the issue with Chloe this afternoon when she visits.

"How are you, Doug?"

"Very good, thanks Chloe. Really pleased with the new mortgages we've got available now, as well."

"You're spot on Doug, and the other advisers are really beginning to sell them to clients. So what's your plan this week?"

"Get some people in to talk to. If I'm honest Chloe…"

"Wouldn't expect anything else from you, Doug…go on -- what's on your mind?"

"It's just that…"

"Go on."

"It's just that when I came for the interview you all said that I'd have lots of people to speak with day in and day out and that my biggest challenge would be to get qualified as soon as possible so I could start to give advice; but, I've got no one to see."

"I see," thought Chloe. "Are you not getting any referrals from the negotiating team out there?"

"One or two…but they're very difficult to get hold of and when I get through on the phone, they just want me to quote some mortgage rates at them and get them the cheapest deal. They don't want to call in."

"I see," continued Chloe. "Hold on and let me nip out for a moment."

I wonder where she's going. Hope I didn't land myself in trouble, but it seriously is quiet and it worries me that I'm not seeing anyone.

"Sorry about that, Doug. Keith's popping in to join our meeting."

Keith Burdett was the office Sales Manager. He wasn't my boss -- that was Chloe, but I sort of had a dotted line to Keith. Keith was alright, really -- a typical slicky estate agent though, brought up in the company and started when he left school. They call him the Silver Fox and he's really a good salesman, with an early head of silvery grey slicked-back hair. Wears a suit everyday with matching handkerchief in his top pocket.

An OK manager, as far as I can see. Everyone looks up to Keith and he tends to be a "lead from the front" manager.

He's in his late 30's, married, no children and is a real petrol head. He adores his BMW 7 Series, which has pride of place in the office car park. Immaculately polished, just like Keith.

I like Keith, but I'm not sure what he thinks of me.

"Hi Keith," I start, when he makes his entrance.

"Hi Doug…Chloe…what's this all about then?"

"Doug…you start…" said Chloe

"Gulp… OK… Let's get to the point." I figured this was the best route. "I've just got no one to see, and its beginning to worry me a tad. I was led to believe that there would be a constant flow of people for me to see and advise, but all I'm getting is a dribble, and those that I'm getting through to don't really want to speak with me. They just want the best mortgage deal quoted over the phone. I'm really frustrated."

"We're just doing what we've always done here, Doug", defended Keith. "We're giving you names to call. Isn't that what you want?" Keith turned to Chloe, as well as me.

Chloe began. "Yes, Keith it is, but it seems we're not having the success we should be having here. It's in all our interests to get this right, would you agree?"

"Absolutely" said Keith. This was one of his favourite words, others were totally, positive, fabuloso, let's do it. Some of the guys have put these words on a bingo sheet and tick them off during the day as a game. Bit harsh that, but funny.

Chloe continued, "What time are you closing tonight, Keith?"

"Tonight, officially 6pm, but we tend to stay a little later if we've got people to see."

"How about we shut up at 5.30pm, get Deidre to man the phones and take any messages and I'll run a referral training session for 30 minutes?"

"Fabuloso," said Keith, as I ticked that one off on the bingo sheet in my head. "I'll set it up, Chloe. Gotta run now; new house to list. See you at 5.30pm."

I glanced at the clock and it read 6.05pm. We'd run over by 5 minutes, but no one minded. The two girls headed out the door to get the bus, Vince remained at his desk and got straight on the phones. I liked Vince, a real East End "Geezer" with a heart of gold. Keith was out the back in a flash, destination – BMW 7 Series with his own plates – KB5 E5T. Reckoned it stood for his name and his profession of ESTate agent. Keith swore that it stood for something else, but wouldn't tell anyone.

Chloe and I settled back in my office and I made her a cup of tea.

"Only got ten minutes now, Doug, before I have to get away, so let's crack on."

"That was excellent Chloe... the training... first class and you got all the guys really pumped up to give me referrals."

"Over to you, Doug. Have you got your Learning Diary? They recommended you use on your training course."

"Yes, I have it here in my brief case."

"Well, why don't you jot down some of the key points that you learned about getting referrals and I'll speak with you tomorrow. I need to speak with Vince before I go."

So I noted relevant points in my diary.

How to get office based referrals

The key to a referral, wherever it comes from, is for it to be delivered as far as possible, on a plate. Giving some one a phone number to ring, is not a referral.

The team should know what problems and customer challenges my advice can solve so that they can tell the customer about me and how I can solve their problems for them.
Some problems and customer challenges I solve are:

- Time –
- Desire for the best deal
- Right mortgage deal
- Protection
- Trust

Once they've established what situation the customer is in and revealed some potential hiccups or problems they have, then they suggest talking with me as I can help to solve this hiccup or problem.

They are to close the customer by suggesting that they have access to my diary now so can fix up an appointment straight away to see me. My job is to make contact with them to further secure the appointment, but be careful that I don't start selling on the phone. I need to be in mind that I need to secure the appointment first and foremost. After dealing with the customer, I must communicate to the team how I did.

Regularly I need to be telling the team about what I can do, new deals, new products, and new services. My advice plugs the problems and challenges that their customer might have. Make a mental note to do some more training with the team every month as they really enjoyed that.

There -- that's done. I do like the idea of keeping a learning diary. It's good to summarise what things I've learned and when I learned them, as well. And the best news is that I can now sit back and wait for all these appointments. Life's good at last.

"I'm just shooting off now, Doug. Did you get your diary filled in?" said Chloe.

"Yep, all done and I'm now looking forward to lots of appointments."

"That's what I wanted to mention, Doug. I mean... do you remember when you took on the job, you did commit to generating your own leads, as well?"

"Yes I did, didn't I? I don't know where to start, Chloe."

"It's called Client Acquisition Strategies now, Doug. Used to be called Prospecting back in the 80's. Listen, have you joined the SPA yet, as I advised?"

"No, but it's on my list, Chloe"

"OK, the reason I asked is that on Thursday evening, they've got a speaker event on at the Station Hotel and the lady is speaking about Client Acquisition Strategies. I reckon that it's going to help you a lot. Are you free Thursday evening?"

"Are you asking me out, Chloe?"

"Stop it, young man; behave yourself. I'm inviting James from Edmonton and Louisa from Hackney to come along, as well. I'll be there. Can you make it, Doug?"

"Yes, I can."

As Chloe left, I thought this sounded fun. I'm not into these networking events, but the speaker sounded good. On the internet that night, I accessed the SPA website. The Society of Professional Advisers had about 20,000 members and local branches around the UK. Every month they had a speaker who would talk about all sorts of things connected with our work. The speaker on Thursday was Melanie Melish, who was a professional speaker and trainer based here in North London. She looked a dish in the photograph, so I thought I'd definitely go along. What did I have to lose, anyway? And I could learn some strategies to get more customers.

A quick flick over to Facebook to see who's around, but I was disturbed by a text coming through. I hope its Jeff. Fancy a few beers tonight and Jeff's always up for it. No, it was from dad asking how I was and why I hadn't phoned in ages. Oh dear, I'm in trouble now.

Never know what to wear at these *do's* so I put on my posh suit. Phoned Vicky this afternoon; she's based in Southampton branch. Since she's so good with people, I thought I'd try to get some ideas about how to network at these events. Vicky was very well; her husband is due back this weekend after a stint at sea. He's serving on a patrol ship that's sweeping along the horn of Africa looking for Somali pirates, so Vicky thinks he'll have a nice suntan. That's got to be a good job – pointing a 50 calibre machine gun at some poor guys in a little boat rocking around the Indian Ocean.

Sure enough Vicky had some great networking ideas, as I expected; so I wrote these down in my Learning Diary.

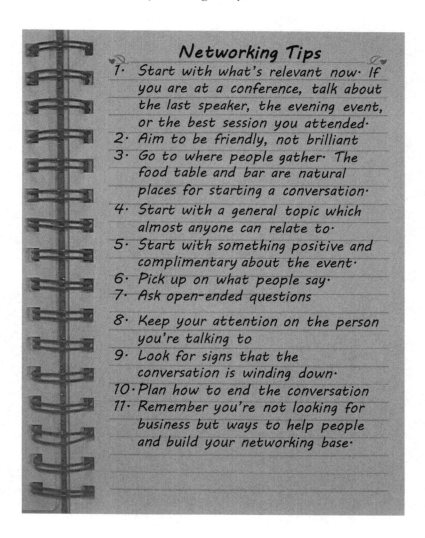

Networking Tips

1. Start with what's relevant now. If you are at a conference, talk about the last speaker, the evening event, or the best session you attended.
2. Aim to be friendly, not brilliant
3. Go to where people gather. The food table and bar are natural places for starting a conversation.
4. Start with a general topic which almost anyone can relate to.
5. Start with something positive and complimentary about the event.
6. Pick up on what people say.
7. Ask open-ended questions
8. Keep your attention on the person you're talking to
9. Look for signs that the conversation is winding down.
10. Plan how to end the conversation
11. Remember you're not looking for business but ways to help people and build your networking base.

I met James in the doorway of the hotel.

"Do you know anyone else here, James, apart from Chloe and Louisa?"

"Nope, although I recognise those fellas over there. There's got to be about 70 or more people here tonight."

"Let's head over to the coffee and biscuits. I could do with a cuppa."

Melanie Melish was being introduced by this rather round man who was the branch Chairman. He looked so old fashioned, moustache, three piece suit, dark, of course. Everyone seemed to be wearing dark clothing. Looking around the room, there appeared to be very few women; I wonder if this is indicative of the financial services industry.

Wow. Melanie was something else -- so full of energy and very entertaining. One day, I'd like to do that. I should make that a goal. I relaxed and began to listen to Melanie.

> "Are you in the business of continually needing to see clients to be successful in your business? Of course you are, unless you're lucky enough to be so well established that business flocks to you.
>
> But most of us need a steady stream of new clients to keep our businesses healthy.
>
> All successful mortgage advisers, IFAs and consultants operate continuous client acquisition strategies to bring in new business. This used to be called prospecting, but that sounds like a gold digger from the Klondike.
>
> Without these strategies in place, your business may well dry up. Even in boom times when you are just so busy, it's easy to take your eye off the ball and not spend time looking for new clients. So let's have a look at the various ways you can do this and run an exercise that'll help you see which method gives you most results and you enjoy most.
>
> I call it your Value/Headache Scale and it's all to do with finding the most suitable source of business for you, personally. First of all, I'd like you to do a little exercise. Up on the screen, you can see that I'm showing a grid with about 15 rows down the left-hand side. I'd like you to work with the people next to you in groups of three and write down in the left hand column all the various ways you've heard of that can be used to get new clients. Go on; have a go and I'll give you five minutes."

I turned to James and a guy on my right whose name badge said Colin Turner.

"Hi Colin. I'm Doug and this is James."

We exchanged pleasantries. I took out my pad and drew Melanie's grid and we started to brainstorm all the different ways we can get new clients. Colin was self employed and so had to prospect. He didn't have the luxury of having an office providing leads, so he came up with some we had never heard of.

Melanie solicited feedback from the whole room and I added some of hers to my list, which looked like this once I got rid of the silly ones such as "beg people in the street", and "ask Santa."

My learning diary looked like this:

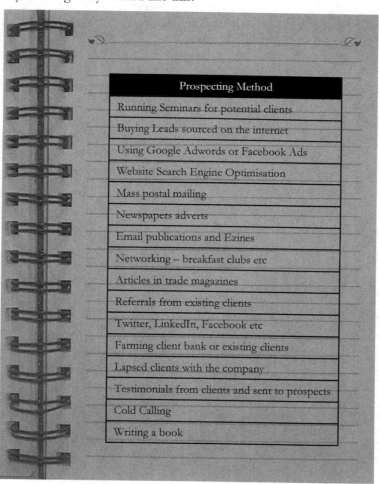

Prospecting Method
Running Seminars for potential clients
Buying Leads sourced on the internet
Using Google Adwords or Facebook Ads
Website Search Engine Optimisation
Mass postal mailing
Newspapers adverts
Email publications and Ezines
Networking – breakfast clubs etc
Articles in trade magazines
Referrals from existing clients
Twitter, LinkedIn, Facebook etc
Farming client bank or existing clients
Lapsed clients with the company
Testimonials from clients and sent to prospects
Cold Calling
Writing a book

Now, where's Melanie going on this I wondered? I needn't wonder any more as the lady took to the stage.

> "Great work everyone. Next, I'd like you to go draw two more columns on your grid, the first one titled "Value" and the second one to the right titled "Headache." Now, go to the first column and award marks out of 10 for how effective it is. For example on most people's lists today we have running seminars, and you might think this is really effective in attracting new clients so you award it 8 out of 10.
>
> In the next column you need to do the same, but this time for how much of a headache doing that method causes you. Taking the seminar route, I'd say this involves a lot of work and hassle. Booking rooms, inviting people, laying on food and refreshments, making sure people turn up, actually doing the talk itself which many people don't like. So you might give this an 8 out of 10 rating. Another one on my list is writing a book. Now you just maybe don't want to do this. The thought of sitting in front of a laptop for hundreds of hours tapping away on the keyboard might turn you completely insane, so you might award this a 10, as it's a major headache.
>
> OK everyone. In the same groups, can you complete the numbers for the Value/Headache scale?"

What a great exercise. This is what my Value/Headache scale looked like at the end.

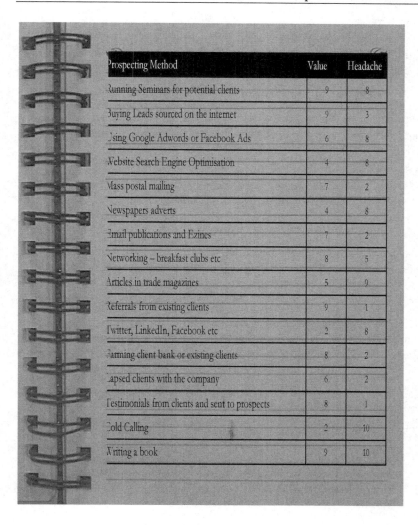

Prospecting Method	Value	Headache
Running Seminars for potential clients	9	8
Buying Leads sourced on the internet	9	3
Using Google Adwords or Facebook Ads	6	8
Website Search Engine Optimisation	4	8
Mass postal mailing	7	2
Newspapers adverts	4	8
Email publications and Ezines	7	2
Networking – breakfast clubs etc	8	5
Articles in trade magazines	5	9
Referrals from existing clients	9	1
Twitter, LinkedIn, Facebook etc	2	8
Farming client bank or existing clients	8	2
Lapsed clients with the company	6	2
Testimonials from clients and sent to prospects	8	1
Cold Calling	2	10
Writing a book	9	10

I could see very clearly that I was looking for a high:low scale for prospecting methods that I should be using to get my own clients. My best routes are buying leads form the internet (so long as Chloe would agree to spend the budget), postal mailings of our client base, weekly emails to our customers, networking, referrals from existing clients, farming the estate agents client base, (which Keith tells me is huge) as the office has been based in the same spot since 1986, with a few owners, but there's a database of everyone who has bought and sold properties since then. Finally, testimonials from happy clients can be used. Cold calling, which I don't really need, is banned.

As I left the meeting, saying goodbye to James at the steps, I began to think about how I could get some more leads, some more customers to give advice. I realised that I was sitting on a goldmine in the form of the office and all those past clients and current clients to phone. I thought about joining the SPA and maybe the local breakfast club to start networking, as well. But my future business lay in the form of that massive client bank.

Louisa didn't make it tonight and nor did Chloe. I wonder why. I must say though, Melanie made an impression on me; I bought her CD that she was selling. I'll listen to that later, after I've ripped it onto my iPod. "The 8 Principles of Making Appointments". Liked her, she was cute, as well.

The next day was a Friday, always busy in the office with contracts being exchanged and completions. I love helping the people who are moving in on a Friday. They're so excited about buying their homes. I was, as well, but I have too many bad memories of Heidi and our place together. Never mind. That's all forgotten now, but I sometimes wonder how she's getting on with that Frenchman.

I didn't have any appointments in the morning -- just two in the afternoon. The team was really doing well since Chloe's training so I was well pleased, but I thought I'd make a start on the database. Keith was very enthusiastic about the idea of my phoning older clients of the agency and asked if I would mention about selling their current home. I agreed to do so.

The database was held in a very old computer programme which you could open via Excel, so it wasn't too difficult gaining access. There were still hundreds of paper files upstairs in the storeroom, as well. But I had to make a start somewhere.

So I picked up the phone and dialled the first number. This couple bought their house from us in 1997, a day after the General Election which brought in Tony Blair as our new Prime Minister. Mr. and Mrs. Brandon. The phone starting ringing...

"Hello, is that Mr. Brandon"

"Speaking"

"Hello, my name is Doug Ballantyne from Harris Estates in the High Street. You bought your home through us in 1997 and I was wondering whether you might want to speak with a financial adviser about reviewing your financial circumstances, having a look at your mortgage and getting a good deal?"

"No thanks, I'm a little busy right now; I'll call you if we need to sell our house. OK?"

Well that was a huge success -- not. Let's try the next one. The phone was ringing...

"Hello, is that Mrs. Charvet?"

"No dear. She moved away five years ago. Sorry."

"OK, sorry to disturb you."

Next one. Richard Greenstead, who bought 23 Amanda Drive.

"Hi, is that Richard Greenstead?"

"Yes, it is. Who's calling please?"

"I'm Doug Ballantyne, from Harris Estates in the High Street. You bought your home through us in 2004 and I was wondering whether you might want to speak with me as I'm a financial adviser and I can review your financial circumstances; maybe look at your mortgage and get a good deal?"

"Not today. Thank you, Doug"

"OK. Sorry to disturb you."

This was not going well, so I thought I'd nip into the kitchen to make everyone a cup of tea. After that, I think I'll get on with some paperwork and file submissions and update my learning diary from last night's meeting. I tell you, this making appointment lark isn't easy.

That evening, I decided to go for a run in Victoria Park, which is just down the road from my flat. It's a great venue and now that the days are getting slightly longer, we have daylight until about 7.30pm. The clocks spring forward this weekend as well, so I can get some regular runs in. I have thought of doing a half marathon or something like that -- probably won't though. Need to put it in my goals.

I ripped Melanie's CD earlier and put it on my iPod. Bought an arm strap from Gizoo.com earlier this week and that arrived this morning so I can listen happily to my music whilst running -- fantastic. But this evening for the next 45 minutes I'm going to listen to Melanie Melish and the "8 Principles of Making Appointments" as I certainly need some help.

"Hi, I'm Melanie Melish talking to you today about the 8 Principles of Making Appointments. The first hurdle is to get in front of your prospects as soon as you can. I'm going to share with you the 8 principles that'll tool you up to be able to make successful calls to fix up an appointment with these people.

Principle number one, activity funnelling

Ask any salesperson what's the secret to success and you'll get the answer – activity. Activity breeds sales so the trick is to target yourself with the right amount of activity to achieve the sales you want to have.

Ask yourself these questions:

How many sales do you need over a given period, such as one month?

How many appointments with customers do you need to generate these sales over the same period?

How many calls do you need to make, over the same period, to generate the desired number of appointments?

Now you need to plot these on the funnel, starting at the bottom with the number of sales you need. Say you need 6 sales per week. Now to generate 6 sales, you need to be sitting in front of 10 people, say. And to generate 10 appointments, you need to be making 16 calls, over the same period. Et voila, you have a sales ratio of 16:10:6. So for every sale, you need to be making between 2 or 3 prospecting calls.

The trick is to start thinking this way. Especially if you don't like making calls, and not many salespeople do. Say to yourself, unless I make 3 calls right now, my sales figures will be down by 1 this week, and this should motivate you to pick up the phone and dial.

The second principle is to chain yourself to your desk for 45 minutes

Making calls to fix up appointments isn't something every salesperson wants to do because you'll get your fair share of refusals and no's. And these don't engender warm snugly feelings. It's not a pleasurable task. And it doesn't keep you fit either.

So the trick is to chain yourself to your desk for 45 minutes and do nothing else but make calls. Otherwise, it's very easy to be distracted to another gratifying task such as checking email or making a cup of tea.

That's where I went wrong yesterday. I gave up after just 3 calls and made myself a cup of tea.

45 minutes is shown to be the optimum timing for making calls – any shorter and you won't get through the calls you have to make and any longer and you begin to lose your sharpness and enthusiasm.

Many salespeople ask me what is the best time to make the calls. That depends much on your body clock and when you think your prospects will be in to receive your call. It's known that from 9 to 11am is the most effective time. Next is 7 to 8pm and the worse time is between 4 and 6pm.

The days, you decide to make your calls must fit around your schedule. Although, we have found Fridays to be not as successful as say a Tuesday because people have an "end of the week" feeling.

The third principle is to sellotape the phone to your wrist

This principle leads on from the last one with the overriding concern being how easily distracted salespeople are (and I put myself in that category as well). The rule to follow is the 60 second rule. When you've hung up on the customer, keep the phone in your hand for a maximum of 60 seconds before you make your next outgoing call.

Not only does this prevent you taking an incoming call but it stops you doing much else apart from making important notes or diary entries with your other hand. Use your left hand to hold the receiver thus freeing up your writing hand unless you're left handed, of course.

Use a stop watch if you like.

And don't be tempted to use a conference facility on your phone so you can use both hands. They differ in quality, so that ensure you get to take a call from someone else using conference facilities to test the quality of your system. Some sound as though you're in the rest room and some have a mini second of silence between you speaking and the other person speaking, which doesn't sound natural.

The fourth principle is 'do not disturb.'

Next time you're in a hotel, grab the "do not disturb" sign and use this when you enter your 45 minutes of calling. Hang it on your back to warn prospective interrupters not to disturb you. Explain to everyone in the office or workplace that you need 45 minutes of uninterrupted time to make your appointments, so can they hold calls and messages until afterwards.

Ensure you have everything to hand before you pick up the phone and start your stopwatch. CRM package opened up, diary ready and pen that works with some note paper ready. And remember to switch off your mobile phone as well.

The fifth principle is to know what it is you sell.

A little obvious, but worth reminding yourself of what it is you aim to achieve with the call. You're after a meeting, either face-to-face or maybe via web conferencing or telephone. You do not want to be sucked into discussing the product or service.

Focus on getting the appointment and you'll be successful.

But you do need to motivate the prospect to want to meet with you and here you need to know what their motivation is. WIIFM – or what's in it for me. What is it that the prospect will buy into – what's the hook or hot button?

Keep the hook enticing and leave out the detail. Make the prospect feel hungry but don't feed them. For a financial services call it might be to save them money, provide security for the future or secure the best finance for them. These sound interesting but don't go into detail.

When probed for more information, explain that this is why meeting them face-to-face is advantageous to you both and you'll be happy to do this for them. Repeat the hot buttons once more.

The sixth principle is to focus on your vocal cosmetics.

Before you pick up the phone, warm up your vocals, maybe with a friendly call to someone else. The keys to your vocals for making appointments are pace, lowering your voice, posture and facial expressions.

Ask someone to feed back on your pace when talking on the phone. If you are a little apprehensive, then you'll find yourself being too fast. In fact, if you speak at the same pace as face-to-face conversation, then you are too fast for the phone. You should slow down on the phone and use more pauses. It's known that if you are quicker than the prospect at talking on the phone, you'll come across as high pressured. Now, polite persistence is one thing, but coming over as high pressured is another.

Lower your voice slightly when making appointments, particularly when you ask for the appointment. Lower voices are more welcoming and warm, but don't go doing a *Barry White*!

Ensure your posture allows for a full breath and for diaphragmatic breathing. Care not to crouch over and push your body towards the computer, as this will crush your diaphragm and prevent you from using your full vocal range. Many people like to stand to make appointments and this is a great tip. Not only does your voice have maximum capacity, but standing also makes you feel more confident.

Finally, your facial expressions can give a warm intention. Smiling and enthusing, maybe using real gestures can have a fantastic affect with your prospect, making you come over as genuine, honest and non-scripted. Being enthusiastic can make sure you operate with a positive attitude, as well and this state of mind is imperative when making appointments.

Seventh is to plan -- don't can.

In every aspect of selling, we follow the golden rule of plan, do, and review. Plan your calling. Some salespeople like to follow a script and this is fine so long as the words are natural and not canned. Unfortunately, scripted, written words just don't always sound right when spoken. For example,

"Can I just spend 5 minutes of your time to explain..."

Sounds very formal but I've seen it on hundreds of scripts. Instead use:

"Could I just walk you through..." or something similar.

Whether you script or not, you do need a plan to follow. The 4 essentials to a successful calling plan are introduction, ice breaker, reason for the call and asking for the appointment. You need some clear words and scripts within each heading and here are some ideas and pointers for you.

Introduction first.

During the first few seconds of the call, you need to mention their name 2 or 3 times as it's known to be the most wonderful thing for someone to hear. Naturally ask for the person by name and when they confirm, repeat it again and thank them. Then introduce yourself using the phrase "this is Melanie Melish from...." Don't say "my name is...." This is so demeaning. After all, President Obama wouldn't say "My name is Barack Obama," would he?

Then you need to say something to get them talking or responding before you follow on. Some salespeople like to ask "how are you today?" -- some don't. You choose. But what this does is begin to break the ice and it can be very brief. This does smell of a telephone canvasser, though.

Care with the "is it convenient to talk" line. If you do use this, you will achieve less appointments and that's a fact. Try using "If it's convenient right now, this is Melanie Melish from ...."

Slightly different but at least you're saying it. Try without saying it. Go on -- I dare you.

Next, breaking the ice.

Before you steam into asking for the appointment, you do need to break the ice a little. This is best achieved using a question. For example, if you're calling a client of your company that has had little contact with you, (known as an orphan client), say "XYZ has asked me to call you about your business with us."

And then pause. Or if it's a referral say: "Has Michael Purffet mentioned my name to you at all recently?"

This last one works really well with cold calling, as well. "Has my name been mentioned to you at all recently?"

Then reason for call.

Await their response and then move onto the benefit statement. In other words, the reason for the call. It's here that you want to use the WIIFMs or hot buttons you determined earlier. Here's an example:

"The reason for my call today, Bob, as you might be aware, is that XYZ has recently developed a service designed to save you money and secure the best finance for people like you and we'd be happy to run this by you."

Notice the absence of the word "I" and the mention of the word "you" 4 times. And there's some hypnotic words in there as well, you saw them, didn't you?

Don't use words such as appointment – this sounds so clinical and reminds me of a dentist.

Finally, ask for appointment.

Finally you ask for the meeting by giving them some suggested dates and times as this allows you to group meetings, especially if you have to travel to the customer. This last bit is not too tricky unless you forget to pause. I've known some salespeople to carry on talking and dig themselves a really big hole in which to fall.

But you wouldn't do that would you?

Finish off by confirming your name and the meeting arrangements and say goodbye.

I've some really good calling scripts that work for referrals, orphan clients, letter follow-ups and cold. Just email me and I'll be happy to ping them over to you.

My last principle today is polite resistance.

I think it's important to not get too hung up with objection handling. If they don't want to see you, then so long as you have enough people to call, move onto the next call.

However, I often think "how would the prospect feel if you didn't try to politely persuade them a little?" They might think that you don't care too much for your service.

Polite resistance is the key at this stage.

Whatever objection handling technique you use, it's important to listen and empathise first. For example:

"That's OK Bob; I do see where you're coming from here. Actually lots of people we phone feel the same as you initially......"

Then just repeat your offering....

"I'm just offering a meeting to talk through the service that'll help you secure the best finance for you and save you money. It'll take just 25 minutes…when might be convenient for you. Bob?"

So there we have our 8 principles to making appointments. I trust I've reminded you of some ideas you already knew but haven't used for some time during the boom years and maybe shared some new tips with you, to help you achieve your revenue targets this year. This is Melanie Melish signing off.

At the end of Melanie's speech I found myself sitting on a park bench catching my breath. I haven't been running for a while and didn't realise how exhausting it can be. But Melanie's 8 principles really rang a bell with me and I could see exactly where I had been going wrong today. I wasn't focusing on the appointment or using ice breakers, or any sort of plan.

Back home I dug out my learning diary and made the following notes:

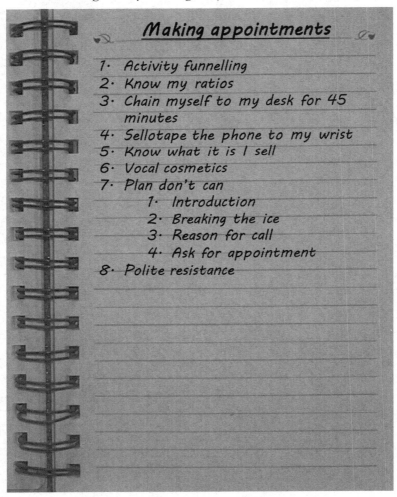

Making appointments

1. Activity funnelling
2. Know my ratios
3. Chain myself to my desk for 45 minutes
4. Sellotape the phone to my wrist
5. Know what it is I sell
6. Vocal cosmetics
7. Plan don't can
   1. Introduction
   2. Breaking the ice
   3. Reason for call
   4. Ask for appointment
8. Polite resistance

World, just wait until tomorrow…

Chapter 4 – Please like me

In which Doug learns how to give a great first impression and really understands rapport building

Sure enough my appointment making was a real hit and very soon my diary was filling up nicely. The team was supplying leads and making appointments straight into my diary. This is easy now, as all our diaries are online and everyone can see and add to them. Even when the guys are out visiting vendors and customers, they can access my diary via their iPads and iPhones. Really cool.

I've also been adding to the number of people in my diary by making calls to past customers of the agency. The big difference is following a structure and focusing on selling the appointment rather than products and advice over the phone.

Chloe's really pleased for me and genuinely so, as well. She shows real empathy and always wants to help me. This afternoon she's observing me during my last client meeting. It's for a couple who have just put their house on the market with us.

I'm actually quite nervous, being watched.

"Two saccharines please, Doug" said Chloe.

"No problem. I think we've got some in the cupboard as the part-timers use them".

Chloe was looking very professional today, a new business suit I think, all matching and very smart. She was trying to lose some weight as one of her best friends was getting married, for the second time soon and Chloe was going to be an honoured guest or something. I didn't really understand all the ins and outs of wedding etiquette. Personally, I thought Chloe was slim anyway. Women always want to be skinnier. I guess I'll never understand.

As I glanced at my waistline, I promised myself to go for a run this evening.

"So Doug, how do you think the meeting went?"

"OK, I guess. They've both got plenty of information about what I can do to help them, and some quotes, too. I think we got along alright, as well."

Chloe said nothing, and being a paid up member of the "if there's silence, I'll fill it club," I filled it.

"Uhmm I wasn't too impressed with my first impressions. I know that's really important. I think I rushed into it a little too quickly."

"Tell me…what was your objective of the meeting?"

"Uhmmm…to impress them, to show them what I can do for them and all the mortgages I can arrange to give them value of their agency fee."

"Oh. What does that mean, Doug?"

"Keith told me that one. He told me that the vendor pays us 1.25% sole agency fee on their home if it sells. It's on the market for £450,000 so we stand to make over £5,500 in fees. He told me to lay it on so they get a great service from us all."

"Good advice," empathised Chloe. "Tell me, Doug, how do you keep to the sales process they taught you at your Central Sales Training Course?"

"Through habit I suppose. We did loads of role-playing and the trainers thought I was really good. But…"

"But what, Doug?"

"But it's a little different when you're in front of real people, Chloe. Real customers don't stick to the sales process, so I go with the flow somewhat."

"I see what you mean, Doug. You know I see that a lot of new advisers and don't get me wrong, I know you have lots of experience in handling people, but you are new to sales, aren't you?"

"Yes I am, but I'm enjoying it. Tell me it straight, Chloe. What did I do wrong?"

"Come on, Doug. You don't want that, do you?" You were good in there. You demonstrated knowledge of the mortgage market, you showed confidence and professionalism and you looked after the vendors really well. As a tweak, I would say be clear as to your objective before each meeting. I would say the objective you gave me was a little weak…a little vague. I think you would need to tighten this up and then decide how you did measured against that objective."

"OK Chloe, fair play. What do you think my objective should have been?"

"Put yourself in the customer's shoes. What do you think they would want from that meeting?"

"Uhhmm…I guess they would want to know that I'm professional and know my stuff, have confidence in me that I can take care of things for them, trust in me as an adviser, confidence that I have helped people like themselves before, understand their needs."

Exactly, Doug. That's totally what they would have wanted. And what did you give them?"

I paused, thought for a moment. And then I realised where Chloe was going with this. The sales process they gave us at Central Training was based around some solid principles and she was asking me to stick to it. But she didn't tell me, she made me think it through. Clever.

"I guess I gave them a whole lot of information about mortgages, lots of details. But they liked me."

"They did like you Doug. You're a likeable person; that's not in doubt. But there's a difference between liking someone and having trust and a rapport with a professional adviser. I think you were trying too hard to be liked. Don't worry, Doug, many of your colleagues have done the same thing at first. The trick is to change and move forward."

"You're right Chloe."

"But Doug, you did well in there. Those vendors got a great service from you. Keith would be pleased with how you handled them. Just pick up where we left off at your next meeting. Give them a call tomorrow and sell the next meeting. Remember that customers need to be led to the next step. That's why sales processes are so important. They give us direction and we need to give it to customers. It's called signposting. Did they mention that at training?"

"Can't recall."

"It's quite simple really. Lay down your plan with your customer at an early point -- your agenda if you like. And then take them down that road, telling them where you are in the normal process. Customers kind of expect you to be in charge, to show that you've done this before and you can help to solve all their pains and challenges."

She was right. I needed to follow the company's sales process, spend time on rapport, not just making them like me, and lay off giving too much information at the early part of the meeting and tighten up my first impressions. Oh, and remember to signpost as well. Not a lot then. But, hey, I'm still learning so it's OK to make mistakes.

"Thanks, Chloe. That's helped me a lot. Are you back again next Monday?"

"Yes, I'll be with you during the morning. Will you have some meetings for me to sit in on?"

"I've already got two in the diary."

Whilst it was fresh in my mind, I dug out my learning diary and made some notes.

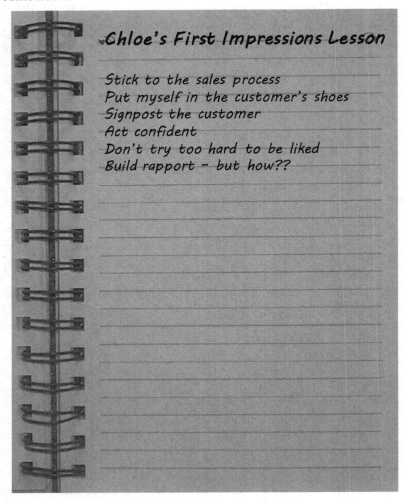

Chloe's First Impressions Lesson

Stick to the sales process
Put myself in the customer's shoes
Signpost the customer
Act confident
Don't try too hard to be liked
Build rapport - but how??

Remember my earlier promise to myself to get a run in before nightfall? I thought I'd sneak out a little early, but just as I was about to flee, Keith's car pulled into the car park at the back. Better say good night and maybe get some feedback from his vendor before I go.

"Hi, Keith. I'm off now; see you in the morning. How'd you get on with the Cooks?"

"Excellent, we've got the listing; I never fail, do I?"

Always very confident was Keith and did it with a smile, so got away with it. He was a good estate agent, though. I thought I'd take the opportunity of getting some more feedback following my meeting, since Chloe's feedback. But let's not be too obvious with Keith.

"Keith, I was wondering, did they get some value from my meeting with them this afternoon?"

"Yes, Doug. They liked you, so good one mate."

Fantastic news, I thought.

"Although Mr. Cook thought you waffled on a little and didn't get to the point quick enough. He's a man of little patience, but Mrs. Cook liked you and told him off in front of me. It was funny to watch."

"Yes, she did keep him in his place at my meeting."

"You need to set out your stall, Doug and stick to it. Would you like a quick lesson from a master of stall setting?"

I assumed Keith meant himself. I thought "What have I to lose?" Remarkable difference between Keith's management style and that of Chloe's, mind you.

"What are you doing, Doug?" asked Keith.

"Heading home."

"No, you're not. You're coming with me for a Master class on stall setting with a prospective new client. I'll introduce you as the mortgage adviser, as well, so we'll get you an appointment, too."

"OK, Keith" I reluctantly agreed.

Keith's car was very comfortable and full of gadgets. He had an in-built Satellite Navigator that was really cool, air-conditioning (of course), bucket seats, MP3 playing stereo. It was a nice set of wheels and Keith was very proud of his car and susceptible to a little compliment.

"Nice car, Keith."

"Yes I think so too. Flattery will get you everywhere, Doug. Anyway-- to action. When I meet these new clients, I'm going to make sure I set out my stall, tell them how we work, show them that we're indispensible and get the listing."

"Sounds good, Keith"

"What do you sell?" continued Keith.

"Mortgages, life assurance, health insurance, house insurance."

"No you don't" said Keith "I've been thinking about this because that's what the previous adviser said and look what happened to her."

"I never knew what happened to the previous adviser -- just that it didn't work out. Apparently, she would speak to hundreds of customers, but hardly anyone bought from her."

"No, I think you're trying to sell a commodity."

"Not with you, Keith."

"You see, a commodity is a product, like this car, like this suit I'm wearing. It's an item that can be sold by a multitude of companies, packaged up and sold cheaper, as well, if you strip out some of the features. This suit I'm wearing came from Next and cost me almost £200, but you can get a suit for £20 from Asda. Admittedly, it's not as nice, but it's a suit."

"Well I don't sell suits, Keith"

"No, you don't, but you treat what you do sell as a commodity, and if you do that Doug, you'll be undercut by someone else. Deirdre would do that and her customers -- my vendors -- just went online to buy the products cheaper because they regarded what she sold as a commodity. They often took out her mortgages, but she hardly ever sold the protection policies, which I know earn you a lot of commission."

"I see what you're saying, Keith, but what do you think I sell?"

"Thought you'd never ask. I think you sell advice, a professional service that helps our clients buy their dream home and ensures that if anything should happen to them, such as death or illness, the home remains theirs forever"

"That's quite good, Keith. I like that."

"You sell a complete home buying financial package that's tailored to the needs of the customer, my vendor. This complements the service we give them. That is, we help them to market and sell their home, which enables them to move and achieve their home buying goals and dreams."

"I like that Keith; it blends the two services together."

"And another thing you should be doing, Doug, is giving the customer a Stall Setter and Reputation Statement outlining how you work and the process you follow."

"Chloe mentioned that earlier."

"There you go, Doug. Keith is the master salesman." boasted Keith.

Good grief, he was on a high. This man was running at maximum octane levels on his own brilliance, but I kind of liked it, it suited his style. Slightly arrogant, but fun as well. After all, Keith had been around the block a few times and knew how to sell houses.

"Tell me more please, Keith."

"A Stall Setter and Reputation Statement is something you give to your customer very early in the meeting once you've broken the ice and begun to build rapport. Then, you want to take control and set out your stall and give the customer a warm feeling about your capabilities. It lasts for no more than 1 minute. I've been doing them for ages and they really work."

"So what goes into them?"

"Let's start with the Stall Setter. It's a bit like an agenda in a meeting. It states the reason for the meeting or appointment. Go over what you'd like to cover, ask for their input and then onto a brief introduction. RUTI is the acronym – R for Reason, U for your stuff, and T for their input and I for introduction"

"That all makes sense, but that's something I kind of talk about anyway with customers."

"Maybe" continued Keith, "But that's the point. You need to polish it, get the words right and make it sound natural. But it needs to be consistent and delivered at the beginning of the meeting."

"How about an example, Keith?"

"OK, but you'll hear it for real with this couple and we've only got 5 minutes before we arrive. Besides, I want to tell you about your Reputation Statement next."

"OK. Thanks for this, by the way"

"That's OK, Doug. I want you to do well as it affects my office revenue. We need your income this year to reach target. Besides, I like to share my expertise in selling."

"I wish you were the trainer from the central course, Keith. You would have done a much better job."

"Yes, I have thought about that as a career move, but I want to make Area Director next."

"Good luck to you, Keith, on that. When I'm Financial Services Director, I'll put in a good word for you."

"Cheers, but let's see about walking before you run. Anyway, we drift – that was your fault. The Reputation Statement is clever as it builds you up in their eyes and launches straight into talking about them and their needs -- especially how they tick. Firstly, say a few words about you and the company who you work for, then something about the type of client you work with to make the customer feel they've come to the right place. Then something that proves how good we are -- maybe a little story about a past customer. Then finally, "Enough of us; let me find out a little more about you."

"How long does that last for?"

"Not long, about 45 seconds max, otherwise you'll bore them and, again, it needs to be practised and polished. Hold on, Doug; here we are. Now these are nice houses on this street. They always sell quickly as they're close to the tube, so we really want this listing. Come on in and watch the master in action."

I had my iPod with me in my jacket pocket so without Keith watching, I pressed record as I was dying to record his Stall Setter and Reputation Statement.

In the car, I jotted down the Stall Setter and Reputation Statement in my Learning Diary as Keith spoke on his hands-free phone.

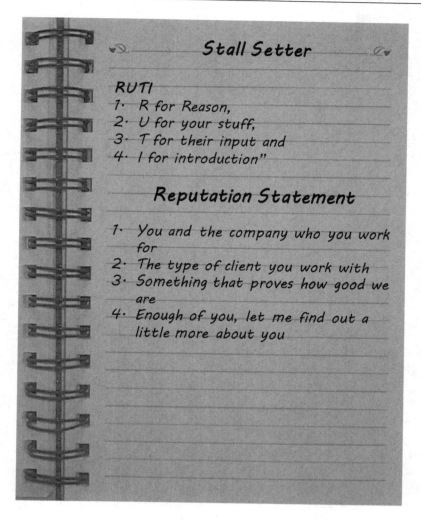

Stall Setter

RUTI
1. R for Reason,
2. U for your stuff,
3. T for their input and
4. I for introduction"

Reputation Statement

1. You and the company who you work for
2. The type of client you work with
3. Something that proves how good we are
4. Enough of you, let me find out a little more about you

Keith dropped me off to my flat, decent of him as it was slightly out of my way and, of course, he got the listing and an appointment for me next week. I reckoned on 45 minutes of daylight left, so I quickly changed into my running gear, strapped my iPod to my arm, and headed out to listen to Keith in action. Pretty slick was Keith, and the couple really liked him. Only 45 minutes available, as I am poised to meet Jeff for a frame of snooker down the club at 8:45pm. Can't be late as he'll never speak with me again.

> "You've decorated your home really beautifully, Mrs. Meadows. Very minimalist and this should appeal to the young professional buyer. Shall we sit down and run through what we would normally do next?"

> "Over here, Keith. I've got some coffee made."

> "The reason for coming here day, following your call, is to talk to you about how we can help you market and sell your home and help you further in your next steps. I'd like to find out more about your plans, if I may, and discuss your thoughts around selling your home and outline what we can offer to achieve your aims. Is there anything else you'd like to talk about today?"

> "Uhm, yes Keith. We'd like to know what you think of the market at the moment and the fees involved. Oh yes, and how much we can realistically get for our place."

> "Ok. We can talk about that."

> "And call me Bob, Keith."

Keith was good and was in total control of the sales process. What had I learned? I picked up that the sales process is there for a reason and can help. Trying to be nice doesn't necessarily build a rapport; it's about being professional and in control. Keith also used a lovely question whilst he was drinking the coffee that had been made for him.

"Bob, can I ask you, what do you look for in a company that's going to sell your home?"

"Uhmm, that's a good question, Keith. I want fairness, honesty and transparency. I want to feel secure that you're doing everything to help me sell."

"Anything else?"

"Value for your fee, I guess."

"That's important isn't it? I'll talk about our fees later but I need to say that we do provide lots of value and this is where Doug comes in. He's our financial expert and can help you sell and buy your new home and make sure that everything is done professionally, easily and without any stress."

Keith later told me that he calls that his criteria question. He asks them what is important to them. He mentioned that most clients go for peace of mind, security, value for money, control… these are known as hot buttons. He reveals their hot button, so he can match the benefits of the service to exactly what they want.

Clever man, Keith.

It was starting to get a little dark so I headed back to my flat. A quick shower and out the door to meet Jeff at the snooker club. I thought I'd grab a burger on the way. I guess I deserved it after the run.

The snooker club was a bit dingy -- upstairs above the old Woolworths in the High Street. An enormous area containing roughly 24 snooker tables, so never a problem to get a table booked for a couple of hours. The place had a slightly sweet smell. We couldn't figure it out and we'd only noticed it shortly after the smoking ban came into effect, anyway.

"I'll break," said Jeff, as he smoothly pushed the cue between his fingers, connected with the white ball which sailed blissfully towards the pack of reds and split them over a space of about a metre square.

"So how's the new job going, Doug?" Jeff and I hadn't really spoken properly for an hour and we now had two hours of quality time to sink a couple of pints and chew the fat. Snooker was a great game to just put the world to rights.

"Going well, thanks, Jeff. Today I had a Masterclass from Keith, the office manager and Chloe, my sales manager."

"Chloe's the one with the nice legs, isn't she Doug?" Typical Jeff, always thinking of one thing.

"I've got a lot of time for Chloe; she's a really good manager and is helping me out loads".

My turn now to pop a red in the corner pocket, followed by the pink, but I missed the red.

"I seem to be trying too hard to make the clients like me, Jeff. Any suggestions? You're really good with customers, especially when you've just met them."

"Thought you'd never ask. You know that Uncle Jeff is always on hand to show you how to handle people. I'm a master of first impressions,"

"Go on, Jeff," as I took to the table with my cue to pot a long distant red.

"First impressions are what count, Doug. You have 90 seconds to make a good first impression, and you know that first impressions last and hardly change. It's where the 90:90 rule comes from. You have 90 seconds to make a first impression and then 90% of that impression lasts." Jeff groaned as my red plopped into the corner pocket and I cued up for the blue.

"So let me tell you what to do for the first 90 seconds. Firstly, you need to act confidently when greeting your customer. Walk slowly and make deliberate movements. That shows confidence. Walk like James Bond towards them, keeping eye contact. As you approach them, stop and move back an inch or so. This tells them sub-consciously that you're non- threatening. Shake their hands like Bill Clinton."

"Who?" I asked.

"The old USA President, a real smooth dude was Bill Clinton and he invented the Bill Clinton handshake. What you do is shake hands with your customer matching exactly the amount of pressure they give you and a maximum of three shakes, then you subtly touch their shoulder with your other hand. Let me show you."

I put the cue down and accepted Jeff's handshake and sure enough he touched my shoulder at the same time. "What does that do, Jeff?"

"It helps to bond and builds rapport. Let me tell you some more; I'm on a roll. Watch the customer's bubble. Don't get too close to them -- about an arm's length is the phrase. If you sit down, try and avoid barriers such as desks or laptops. You need to be facing each other at an angle, rather than head on. Lots of eye contact, but don't stare at a point on their faces."

"Why not, I always stare at the left eye -- always have."

"No Doug, if you do that, then someone will feel uncomfortable with you, and might accuse you of staring. Imagine an egg shape on its side which covers both eyes and their nose and ears. Just move your gaze around this shape and you won't go far wrong, my friend."

"Fantastic stuff Jeff. Any more tips to help me build a rapport?"

"Yep. Smile, Doug, but make the movement to a smile slowly; this looks really genuine. And then, do them a real favour and become interested in them, don't become interesting. I think that was from a Steven Covey book. Be interested, not interesting."

"That's a bit heavy, Jeff; let me think that one through. I get it…don't tell them all about me, find out about them."

"That's right, Doug. Ask some easy questions about them, start learning who they really are and what makes them tick and motivates them, find out their characters, their personalities. Ask the kind of questions that aren't on your factfind form. And above all, Doug, listen to them. Listen and listen some more."

"Your go, Jeff." I missed a sitter there. "Do you want another beer?"

"Yes please, Doug, and when you get back, I'll tell you the real secret to cementing the rapport."

At the bar I noticed two girls had sat down and were chatting to each other. I hadn't seen them in the club before, quite pretty too. But Jeff was waiting so I hurried back to our table.

"I'm all ears, Jeff, go on."

Jeff took a big swig from his pint glass, placed it down carefully and took aim with his cue. A firm thrust with his right arm and the white glided across the green baize towards the last red, and into the corner pocket it went.

"The next thing you need to do, Doug, is to become a little bit like them, but real subtlety is needed here. You see, people like people who are the same as them. That's why we get on, Doug; we're pretty similar. We like the same things.... snooker, girls, beer. We wear similar clothes and talk about the same things. We have good rapport. Would you agree?"

"Certainly would, Jeff. What's your point?"

"You see, we stumbled across each other at work and got on because we are the same in many ways. The secret here is to become a little bit more like your customer, kind of have the same personality as them. Get out of your ego and get into theirs."

"That's harsh, Jeff, I don't have a big ego."

"No, you don't, but you have to stop thinking about yourself and think about the customer. If they're really pacey people, you know, they run off high powered Duracell batteries, and then you need to speed up. If they're really relaxed then you need to slow down. Match their personality a little, Doug and you'll build a rapport. Some people go over the top with this and start to match body languages, gestures, voice, pace and volume. Some people even use similar words as the customer. These things all work, Doug, but you need to be more subtle. Otherwise, you'll end up mimicking them, and that's not good."

"Fascinating stuff, Jeff. Where did you learn all this?"

"Life's little lessons, Doug. Life's little lessons. And talking about life's lessons, have you noticed those two girls at the bar. They keep looking over. We need to take some action here."

"Nice one, Jeff, let me get all those *90 seconds* things sorted in my head first because I'd like to practice them on those girls. OK, here goes. James Bond, move backwards, egg shape eye contact, smile, Bill Clinton, no barriers, ask questions, be interested -- not interesting, match their personality."

"You got it, Doug? Come on. Let's go say *hello.*"

We sauntered across slowly, James Bond style.

The following night I was to meet up with Cheryl. She was the cute one from the snooker club and we'd got on so well that we agreed to go for a meal the very next evening. Nothing fancy; a pizza and we'd see how we got along. Jeff's first impression hints had obviously worked at the club and now I was going to do his last tip – be interested, not interesting – with Cheryl.

A quick note in my learning diary before bed.

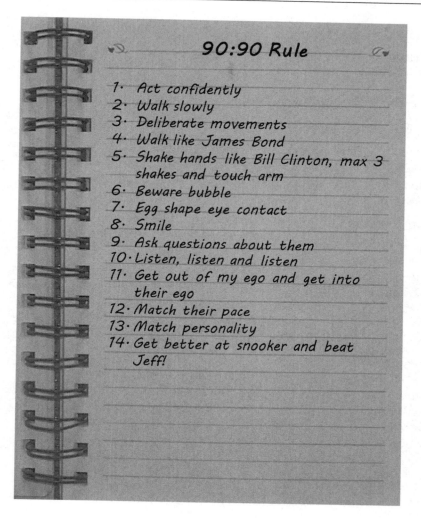

90:90 Rule

1. Act confidently
2. Walk slowly
3. Deliberate movements
4. Walk like James Bond
5. Shake hands like Bill Clinton, max 3 shakes and touch arm
6. Beware bubble
7. Egg shape eye contact
8. Smile
9. Ask questions about them
10. Listen, listen and listen
11. Get out of my ego and get into their ego
12. Match their pace
13. Match personality
14. Get better at snooker and beat Jeff!

Chapter 5 – Just listen please

In which Doug learns the secret of real listening

"Shall we go out again this weekend?" I asked Cheryl.

"I'll text you," she defended. Never a good sign. "What's up, Cheryl?" I asked. "OK. I'll be honest Doug. You're a nice bloke, but I felt like you were trying too hard. I felt like I was being interrogated in the restaurant; it wasn't nice. Sorry, Doug."

Gulp, I've blown it. All I was trying to do was be interested in Cheryl -- Find out about her and her interests. She said interrogation. How awful.

It all started to resonate a little in my head, as I drifted to the bus stop to catch the 73 back to my flat. Keith had said I'd waffled too much. Jeff talked about rapport building and becoming like the customer. Surely I did this with Cheryl. And Chloe, she asks really good questions. She's calling in tomorrow. I'll ask her how she does it. But I've had enough now. Time for home.

I jumped off the 73 bus and strolled towards my flat. It was quite late now and pretty cold, too for a spring night -- a spot of rain in the air. As I strode into my flat, I thought I'd just check out who was online and make myself a cup of tea. This new Facebook app was clever. You can talk to your friends who are online using video, very cool. Couple of friend requests; I'll acknowledge those. I don't think I'll be asking Cheryl to be a friend on Facebook now. She really hurt my feelings, but such is life.

Hold on. Vicky's online. What's she doing up so late? It's almost midnight.

"Hi Vicky, hoz u?" I typed.

It took a little while before she replied. "Hi Doug. I'm OK, how're you?"

"I'm good thanks, Vicky. You're up late?"

"It is late, but early morning in the Pacific where my fiancée is stationed. I was trying to contact him on Facebook, but the military seemed to have blocked it. The last I heard, there was a big mission about to start, but I don't know anymore."

"Are you OK, Vicky?"

"Yes, I'm fine Doug. Don't worry about me. So what you been up to then?"

"Busy. Trying to earn a living. I'm really enjoying the job. What about you?"

"Busy Doug, always busy… Listen Doug, I need sleep, night x."

"Night, Vicky"

I'd never got an "x" from Vicky before. Hey, my bro's online now. It's early evening in Chicago.

"Hey Bro, how's things?"

"Hey Doug, good thanks. Have you spoken to the folks recently?"

"No, I haven't."

"How's the job going, Doug?"

"OK, Steve. Now I have all the technical knowledge I need to learn how to actually sell. This week I've been looking at rapport building and the *first 90 seconds'* first impression. All good stuff."

"Doug, you need to check out a guy called Allan Pease on YouTube. He's the champion of body language."

"Thanks Steve I will, but it's late, need bed."

"Night Bro."

Allan Pease, I'll look him up later. Steve always recommends good sources.

The next morning. I woke up alert and since the mornings were much lighter now, I thought I'd head out for a run in the park. Chloe was due over at the office this morning so I wanted to be fresh for her. I was given some advice a while ago, that if you do some exercise before the day starts, you operate at better performance all day. It seems to work, but it's hard to get up an hour earlier than normal.

"So what do you want to focus on today, Doug?"

"I've always admired how you ask questions, Chloe, and I think I need to sharpen up in that area."

"Ok, what did they teach you at central training?"

"Uhm…open and closed questions. Questions are the answer, the trainer kept going on about. But if I'm honest Chloe, I was more worried about passing my exams at the time so didn't remember much of it."

"So what's the difference between an open and closed question, Doug?"

"That's easy. Open questions get more of an answer; closed questions tend to get a yes or no answer."

"That's right, Doug. Let's head into the meeting room shall we? I feel a training session coming on."

"Cool."

I did admire Chloe. She was always trying to help us and make us better at selling. She once said that it was her job to achieve her area's sales targets through the efforts of her sales team. Chloe really did this and wasn't the kind of dashboard manager who operates from their desk and phone.

We dragged a flipchart into the room and Chloe got into her stride.

"There are a few types of questions that you should be actively using, Doug and you want to be conscious of being able to use them at will. We know about open questions and closed ones."

Chloe wrote them on the flipchart.

"Rudyard Kipling wrote a poem which went like this. I have six honest serving men; they taught me all I knew. Their names are what, why, when, how, where and who. These, Doug, are how you ask open questions."

"The W's."

"That's right, Doug. A couple of other things for you on this. Keep your questions short and sweet. Be careful of machine gun questions where you rattle off three or more questions all in the same string. They're dangerous and just confuse customers."

"OK, I think I might be doing that."

"Well stop yourself, Doug. Also try to sugar coat your questions so you don't sound like you're interrogating your customer. Use "tell me" at the beginning of the sentence or "may I ask", something to soften or sugar coat the question. Make it a conversation, Doug -- not an interrogation."

My mind went straight back to Cheryl and our first and last date.

"And if you feel OK, try to lift your tone a little so that it sounds like a curious question."

"I'll try, Chloe," my mind still on Cheryl. That's where I went wrong. I kept asking machine gun questions, one after the other and I didn't turn it into a conversation.

"The other types of questions you can ask, Doug are probes, which dig deeper into a subject. Imagine a funnel, where your first question opens up some information from your customer. Then you ask follow up questions or probes to find out more. You gradually drift down the funnel until you have the information you want."

"That's clever. I guess I'd need to question funnel quite a few areas of the customer's needs?"

"Yes, Doug. Use nods as well. Verbal nods are things like yes, I see, uh hur... Non verbal nods are when you smile, give eye contact, tilt your head -- that sort of thing. Also pause, Doug. How do you cope with silence with customers?"

"I hate silence and I'll always try to fill it if I can."

"That's where you could really improve, Doug. I call them silent seconds. Enjoy them, relish them and let your customer fill them in. They'll give you enormous extra amounts of information."

"OK, I'll try, but that's a lifetime habit to change."

"Finally Doug, do summarise or playback what you hear occasionally. Sometimes it's useful to repeat the last word or paraphrase a sentence just to listen some more. OK, time to practice. I've written the question types on the flipchart, I'm going to start by asking you some questions about something and we'll note down the types of questions I use. Then you can ask me questions about anything, and I'll keep an eye on the type of questions you use."

"Can I just photo the flipchart for my Learning Diary first."

OK, I'm ready now. Ask away."

"I've got to know you quite well so far this year, Doug, but it would be great if I knew a little more about you, if you don't mind?"

"Fire away, Chloe."

"Can I ask, Doug, what you like to do outside of work?"

"I like to relax, play some snooker. I have a few friends in the area, go for runs…"

"Ur hur, go on…"

"I go online to talk to friends, but I do like to work, as well."

"How are your family, Doug?"

"All well. My big brother lives in the USA. I haven't spoken to my folks for ages."

"How about close friends in London?"

"I've got a couple of pals."

Chloe just looked at me and smiled, silent seconds she said and it was working. I knew what she was getting at.

"No one special in my life yet, Chloe… I was engaged a little while ago, actually 3 years' ago."

"I'm interested, Doug. Do you mind me asking what happened?"

"Long story… she met someone else whilst we were on holiday in France… the surfing instructor… but it was a long time ago."

"I'm sorry to hear that Doug. You must have been devastated?"

"I was pretty upset at the time, but it's in the past. We keep in touch, she's on my Facebook."

"Ah Facebook, there's an enigma. I use LinkedIn. It's so much more professional. My husband scoffs at me for not using Facebook; he uses it for his business."

"What does he do, Chloe?"

"He's an IFA and has his own business -- works from home and uses technology a lot to run his business. He's very clever with it all. So Doug, did you notice the type of questioning I used?"

"Yes, I did. Lots of open questions, loads of sugar coating, non verbal nods and verbal ones, too. And if I'm honest Chloe, the subject was quite personal?"

"Yes Doug, but we often get quite personal with our customers when we're finding out about them, their hopes, fears, trepidations and such, so sugar coating is so important. Also if we measured the amount of talking, you probably spoke about 80% of the time and me about 20%. That's good old Pareto's Law rearing its head again."

"Chloe, I think my appointment has arrived early, I can see them at the front talking to Vince. Shall we pop out and meet them?"

"OK, and I'll watch your meeting, Doug, and give you some feedback on how you ask questions."

As we walked into the foyer area to shake hands with the customers, I remembered James Bond and walked slowly and confidently, remembering to step back an inch to show non-aggression. All this stuff was working.

"Oh Doug, I almost forgot", said Chloe with a little twinkle in her eye. "Louisa from Hackney was asking about you."

Straight after work I headed to the gym. Need to do some serious training now with the London Marathon in mind. Keith recommended the gym. It was a good price and not full of all the posers you get in big chain gyms. I took my iPod because I wanted to listen to some podcasts; now I was regularly synchronising the player with iTunes. The Advanced Selling podcast was my favourite and the Rapport Sellers Weekly Tips, as well.

Five minutes into my treadmill run, my battery gave way, so I removed my earphones and without anything to listen to, my mind wandered. Running on the treadmill is so boring, nothing to do.

I asked myself, what am I doing this for? Fitness, relaxing, but what's my goal?

The guy next to me switched on the TV over head. On the screen was a replay of the New York Marathon and it came to me in that instant. I should enter the London Marathon – that's my goal and this gave me renewed energy to speed up my running on the treadmill.

Channels change at lightning speed in gyms and on came the music channel. A new Indie Band was performing live. Good sound, I thought. What was the band called? Go naked…what a cool name. I'll look them up when I get home.

I finished a good hour in the gym, showered and headed back to my flat with the intention of having something to eat, check out that new band on YouTube and look up Allan Pease. On my way back, I began to think about Heidi in France. Chloe had opened a wound back there for all the best intentions I guess. I wonder how Heidi and Alain were getting on. And what did Chloe mean about Louisa asking after me?... sounds interesting.

As I opened the front door to my flat I almost fell over Reg, who was reaching down to get the post. You see, I share the entrance and corridor with my next door neighbour, Reg. "How's it going ,Doug?"

Reg was born and bred North London and had a thick accent. He was a "diamond geezer" but did remind me of one of the Cray Twins -- same voice, same look. He was a thick set man, around 45 years old, a boxer's nose by the look of it, married to Dawn and had always lived in the flat next to mine. I liked Reg. He'd looked after me when I moved in, told me where everything was and said if I'd got into any bother to come see him. I had no idea what he did for a living, probably a bouncer or a bailiff.

"Hey Doug, what you doing this Sunday?"

"Nothing Reg, nothing planned."

I almost forgot it was Easter Sunday this weekend and I'd have nothing planned. Everyone was heading back to family; Jeff was speeding up the M1 to see his folks. And I had no one close to me, as I'd spilled out to Chloe that day.

"Dawn's cooking up a roast -- beef I think. I noticed you were on your own, Doug. Fancy coming for dinner, just bring some beer around and we'll have a relaxing afternoon."

Now I hadn't had a decent roast dinner in ages and roast beef can't be beaten. And I can get to know Dawn and Reg a little better. "Fantastic Reg, I'd love to."

"See you around noon then, Doug" and with that, Reg headed out into the dark night. I wondered what he did for a living.

YouTube is a fabulous resource; you can watch a video on anything you want. I put in 'Go Naked' and was returned with a number of videos from the band, but one clip caught my eye. It was from an American guy, so I clicked on it and sure enough his name was Bud Clever from South Carolina and he looked like one of these motivational speaker dudes.

Bud started talking "Go naked is my saying for all you salespeople out there who just keep bombarding your customers with just too much stuff. You know how you say too much, use too many brochures, factfinds, leaflets, laptop screens. You just simply lose the focus on your customer with too many things going on. So my advice to you all is to go naked, not without clothes, although that could be fun."

He laughed at that point with a beautiful southern drool.

> "No, seriously. Don't take anything with you next time you go
> see your customer and I guarantee you'll focus your entire
> attention on your customer, where it should be. You'll watch
> them more, ask them more questions, keep your attention on
> them and have a real meaningful conversation. So remember
> everyone, go naked in your next sales meeting. This is Bud
> signing off, y'all."

Gee, he was full of energy; I do love speakers like that. And this go naked idea is excellent.

I fixed myself an omelette, cheese and bacon, with tomato sauce. As I tucked in, I keyed in Allan Pease and found an HD video of him speaking to an audience on body language. So I put the video on full screen, turned up the volume and watched and listened to the Australian fella.

> "G'day, everyone."

Yes he spoke like that. Allan was a loud Australian, very funny, a real comedian, and he ran a training business in Australia. I paused the video, flicked over to Facebook, looked him up, befriended him, popped over to iTunes, signed up for his podcast, then over to his blog, allanpease.com and RSS'd his blog. Then back to the video to watch the rest.

> "I'd like to talk to you folks about body language," he began.
> "The body never lies and us humans have evolved to display and
> read countless signals through our body language. Now, don't
> get wrapped up in single gestures like crossing your arms; I want
> you to look out for combinations of gestures and learn to read
> your customer's language. And look for congruence in the words
> and the body language to make sure they're telling you the truth.

> I want you to watch your customer's body language to make sure
> they're getting along with you, look for positive signs such as
> openness, hands stretched out, palms open, leaning towards you,
> eye contact. One thing I want you to know about is leakage.
> Leakage is where both you and your customer leak your thoughts
> through a sudden change in body language. Watch your
> customer's normal body language and if you see a sudden change,
> you've observed leakage. This could be dangerous. Let's say you
> ask them to go ahead with your product and they suddenly
> change their body language to a negative state, show leakage.
> Then you know there's something wrong. So you can ask them.

> Watch your own leakage as well, customers can read this and
> make opinions. Remember to always show positive body

65

language to make a great impression and beware of negative signals."

And then he showed a brilliant body language model on the screen, I paused the video, did a screen grab, printed it out and glued it into my learning diary and jotted down the other things he mentioned:

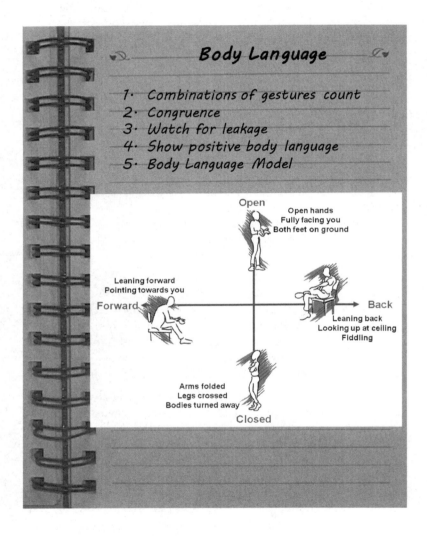

Come on Allan, tell me about this model?

"We need to keep our own body language in the forward open zone, but we need to match their body language to keep rapport.

It was a useful way to see what the customer is thinking about, kind of like a buying signal."

Sunday came around swiftly, and with my crate of Stella Lager, I knocked on Reg's door. I could smell the roast beef cooking, it was a childhood memory of past roast dinners. Reg opened the door.

"Hi Doug… Dawn, we're over to the Kings Head… When do you want us back?"

I could hear the mumble from Dawn, whom I'd never met her before. I imagined a large bouncy woman with massive bouffant of hair. And I couldn't have been further from the truth when Dawn came to the door in her apron.

She was about 5 foot nothing, very slim, and attractive, dark hair with a broad smile underneath fashionable glasses. "Dinner's at 2 o'clock. Don't be late, you two. Otherwise you'll spoil the dinner."

"No problem, Dawn babes, see you later."

The Kings Head was next door to the Pie and Mash shop on the High Street. It was a very old pub, probably three hundred years' old and I guess, my local. Jeff and I had a pint here a few weeks ago, but it wasn't our scene. Reg was at home here and everyone knew him. We settled at the bar on two antique bar stools.

"What you having, Reg?"

"A pint of Old Speckled Hen please, Doug"

My choice of bringing a crate of Stella was obviously incorrect for the situation, so I thought I'd get some takeaways from here for dinner.

The governor came over. "What can I get you gents?"

We sipped our beers as I admired the décor.

"The old place has been around a while. This part of town was famous for its ammunition and gun factories, which is why you can see all the old guns around the walls and pictures of the stuff the armament factory used to make."

"What happened to the factory. Reg?"

"Completely obliterated in the war, amongst most of the houses around here. Before my time though. So how you settling in, Doug?"

"Really well, thanks, Reg."

"You work down at the agency now, don't you?"

"Yes I do… I help customers…"

I paused. Now's my chance to do my value proposition Keith had taught me and see if it really works. "I help the customers who buy and sell homes through the agency. I help them to finance their new home, get some good interest rates and help them to protect their home so if anything happens… like death, illness, a fire… they get to keep their home. You know, take away their worries."

"That sounds great, Doug. Dawn and I have rented that flat since we got married; no need to buy anything. I couldn't afford it anyway."

"Reg, do you mind me asking… what do you do?"

My sugar coating was first class and Reg was not taken back at all. My questioning was getting quite good.

"I work for the Samaritans."

Now that almost knocked me off my stall. I wasn't expecting that.

"Really, Reg, that's interesting. Tell me more?"

Lunch was excellent, the beef was succulent, the roast potatoes just how I like them and for desert, cheesecake, my favourite. Because it was Easter, Reg, Dawn and I tasted some French Brandy, my absolute favourite.

I found out that Reg was Head of Training at the Samaritans, was a total expert at counselling and especially listening. I'd asked about some listening tips, and he said he'd tell me about SAP, which he teaches all new volunteers to the Samaritans. But only when we'd finished lunch.

"So Reg, what's this SAP technique? I'm really curious."

Reg took a sip from his brandy, "Ah yes, SAP. Let me tell you how this works. You see, the problem that most people have when they're listening is they're not actually doing that. Not listening. Most of us are processing what the person is saying and thinking about what we're going to say next. Do you do that, Doug?"

"I do, actually. I'm often thinking about my next question, or trying to make head or tail as to what they're saying."

"That's my point, you see. We're not actually listening to what the other person is saying. We're just waiting for our turn to talk, which makes us interrupt, or butt in. Not good for listening. So we teach our new volunteers to stop thinking about what the other person is saying, trust in their ability to actually hear what's being said, don't inject or give opinions, or even think about what to say next. We help them to love silence."

That brought back Chloe's Silent Seconds.

"So that's the S in SAP then, Reg?"

"Yes. What's your take on it, Doug?"

"You say that we're to stop thinking about what the customer is saying, stop churning it around in my head, stop thinking about what I'm going to say next. That's tough. Reg, what happens if I miss something?"

"Ah, that comes later. Don't worry. If you just let them talk, they'll repeat things, rewind. It's what people do when they're given the space to talk. Trust in your ability to hear what's being said and try to look beyond just the words."

"And the A Reg -- what does that stand for?"

"A stands for appreciate them. Here you do whatever it takes to make the customer aware that they are being listened to and that you are giving them your 100% attention. I noticed you give strong eye contact, Doug. That's good, but beware you don't stare."

"I was told about the egg shape around the eyes and ears. How else could I appreciate the customer?"

Verbal nodding works, give thinking gestures such as hand to chin, look up occasionally to show you're thinking about what they're saying. All the usual stuff like smiling, using your expressions. Do you know why humans have eye brows, Doug?"

"I guess to stop the sweat going from into the eyes."

"That's another benefit. No, the real reason is communication. Your eye brows communicate thousands of feelings and meanings. Try it"

And with that, Reg started to move around his eyebrows as if they were independent of his face. Dawn laughed out loud.

"But that doesn't help you on the phone, Reg…"

"No it doesn't, but a smile and facial expressions come out in the voice, believe me. Also, verbal nods need to happen here, to tell the customer that we're appreciating them. But the final missing piece is the P."

"Go on, Reg."

"P stands for playback and this is simply your playback as to what you've just heard them say, in your words, short and precise, and asking whether this is correct. Don't take the lead here, either, with a question. Once you've played it back, the customer often then just carries on, which is the intention. So there we have SAP – stop thinking, appreciate them, playback."

"Fantastic, Reg. I like that, and I can see this working at your place because you're offering counselling, but what about at my work?"

"You know your work better than me, Doug. Where do you think you could SAP your customers? Are there any sensitive moments?"

"Yes lots. I get really embarrassed when I talk about dying and becoming ill, repossession of homes and that sort of thing. It would work there, wouldn't it? I'm certainly going to do the S and the A, Reg, I need to stop thinking about it and working out my next question. And a short playback would work occasionally, too. Thanks, Reg."

We retired to the front room, brandies in hand. Dawn and I loaded the dishwasher first and I said how wonderful the meal was. "Anytime Doug, you're our neighbour and Reg has taken a shine to you, you can tell."

We watched a movie on Reg's 42-inch flat screen TV -- what a beauty and he had it bolted to the wall. The movie was my favourite of all time – Michael Caine in the original Italian Job. Reg was convinced he knew how to get the gold off the coach at the end. "Easy," he said. "Empty out the fuel tank, which is at the back of the coach, and the weight reduction will stop the coach veering over the edge and will allow you to get the gold". Well that was outside the box. Maybe the brandies helped.

I was dying to try out SAP and I knew that it wouldn't be too long for my chance, but too many brandies sent me to an early bed. I'll write up my diary in the morning.

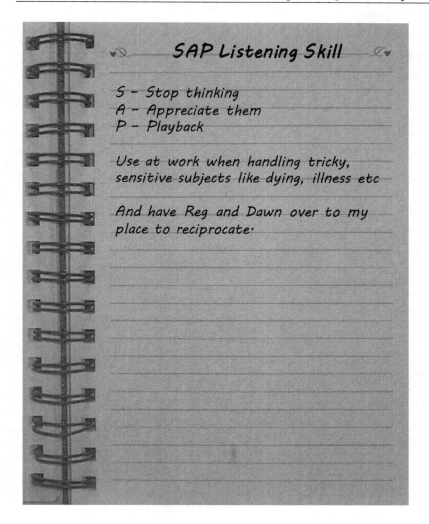

SAP Listening Skill

S - Stop thinking
A - Appreciate them
P - Playback

Use at work when handling tricky, sensitive subjects like dying, illness etc

And have Reg and Dawn over to my place to reciprocate.

Chapter 6 – You're boring me

In which Doug learns about different strokes for different folks

I woke early, cup of strong coffee to nurse my hangover, and a fresh morning run would wake me up properly. The park was deserted apart from a few dog walkers and the sun peering through the morning clouds. Today was a chill out day for me with a trip to the Imperial War Museum, which I'd been promising myself for weeks.

Being on your own in London on a Bank Holiday is strange. Although there are millions of people around you, you get a sense of isolation. Odd that. I was rescued by a text. It was from Vicky. "Doug, if you're available, please call".

So I phoned her straight away on my mobile and flicked it to video call. Vicky answered the call. I could see clearly on my iPhone that she'd been crying. Her mascara was running down her face.

"Vicky, are you OK?" I stupidly asked. Of course, she wasn't, but what else was I to ask?

"No Doug, it's my fiancée. He's been reported missing."

"Vicky, I'm sorry, so sorry" and then I thought I need to do some SAP here. After all I had no other ideas, and being a shoulder to cry on was not my favourite occupation, especially on the phone. I sat down at the nearest bench, next to a couple of Japanese tourists, beneath a blossoming beech tree and I went into SAP mode.

The following morning, I awoke fresh. The chill out day had done the job. As I sipped my first coffee of the morning at my desk, my phone buzzed with an incoming text; it was from Vicky. "Thanks for listening yesterday Doug. You were an angel x."

So the SAP did work. Boy, it was hard. The trickiest part was to stop thinking about what she was saying, and playing back without being over the top. Poor Vicky. It looks like her boyfriend went down fighting -- special ops.

What a hero, though. In the corner of my eye, I spotted Keith. He was late, not like Keith. I'd been in since 8 o'clock as I knew the day after Easter weekend would be very busy with calls and offers being made on houses we were selling. Easter was always the busiest time of the year and this weekend was no exception.

"How're things, Doug?" asked Keith

"Great thanks, Keith. Had a few calls already. Mrs. Turpin wants you to call back. She thinks the couple we sent over are really interested."

"OK Doug. Thanks for taking the message."

By late morning, my diary was filling up nicely and I had appointments until 7 that night. All from applicants who'd made offers on properties and wanted their finances wrapped up quickly. I was on a roll with my questioning and verbal nodding. It seemed like the customers were doing all the talking. But action was needed today with my customers. They needed lots of explanations about mortgages, life assurance and house insurance. It seemed as though I was repeating myself time after time, or that's what it felt like to me. I'm sure my customers liked it. They seemed to understand me. Or I thought so until Keith landed me on the nose later that evening in the pub when we enjoyed a swift half.

"Cricky, Doug. You don't half go on in your interviews, do you?"

I spluttered in my beer "You what Keith?" Now Keith wasn't a man to mince his words. He tended to say what he thought, which is very dangerous with sensitive salespeople, like me.

"This evening, I spoke to two of the applicants you interviewed during the afternoon, just to get some feedback. They liked you, Doug, and felt you were in control, had good structure to your meetings, acted professionally and knowledgeably... "

"But..." I whispered.

"They just got lost. Felt you just kept talking at them and you ended up confusing them, Doug. Don't worry -- they're still going ahead, because they trust you, but I'd sort it out if I were you. I've always said you go on too much."

"Well thanks, Keith, for the feedback" I lied, sipping my beer.

"Anyway, are you watching the Champions League tonight? I Reckon Manchester is going to thrash Barca. What do you think, Doug?"

Now my mind wasn't exactly on the Barca match -- more on trying to do something about the feedback Keith had just shot me with. "Uhm, yes Keith, I think it'll be a good match."

Consumed with the issue at hand, I wandered back to my flat, grabbed a burger from the takeaway. I wasn't too worried about nutritional value at that time. Indoors I logged onto my laptop to check email. I quickly scanned all the usual emails. One forwarded from Louisa of Hackney branch. It was from the SPA, Society of Professional Advisers. There was a meeting this Thursday and Louisa had sent it to me as she and James were attending. She wrote:

"Doug, you coming? James and I are going. Looks like a great meeting on how to sell to different types of people using the colours model."

I wasn't doing anything this Thursday. As a matter of fact, I wasn't doing much most evenings these days, so I replied:

"Louisa thanks -- I'll be there -- see you around 7.30pm."

And the rest of the evening was spent surfing the internet and catching glimpses of Manchester beating Barca 4:0 -- a great victory, with Wayne Rooney scoring a hat-trick.

We'd all come straight from work and met in the foyer of the hotel. The meeting was in the conference hall upstairs and they were expecting almost a hundred people. The atmosphere was electric. After fetching a coffee, we sat down in time for the Chairman to introduce tonight's speaker. I sat next to Louisa as the Chairman announced Mike Lefarge on the stage.

Mike was obviously a very professional and exciting speaker who introduced us to a model of people using four colours.

> "The benefit of the colours, is that you can very quickly gauge your customer's colour or combinations of colours and instantly you know what it is that drives them, motivates them. You see the difference with the colours is that it shows the values of people, what propels them to do what they do. It's not about character, but deeper than that. It looks at the inner drive of your customers.
>
> And when you know that, you can handle them uniquely, sell to them more effectively and communicate in the way they want to be communicated. Use the right language and tactics with them to speed the sale to a successful conclusion."

Now I was sold on this; I wanted to know more and listen to Mike all night. As Mike explained the four colours, I rapidly jotted down notes in my learning diary to capture everything he was saying.

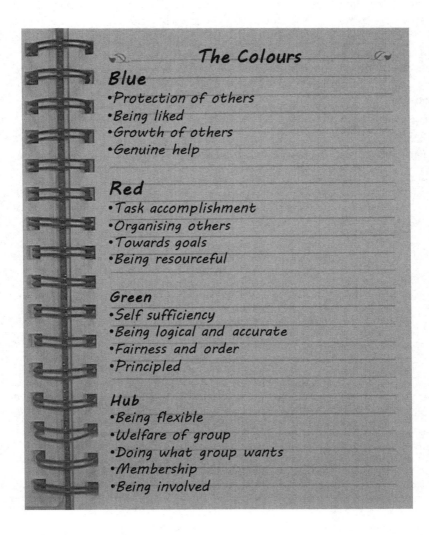

The Colours

Blue
- Protection of others
- Being liked
- Growth of others
- Genuine help

Red
- Task accomplishment
- Organising others
- Towards goals
- Being resourceful

Green
- Self sufficiency
- Being logical and accurate
- Fairness and order
- Principled

Hub
- Being flexible
- Welfare of group
- Doing what group wants
- Membership
- Being involved

Next, Mike had us all move around the room to gather in our coloured groups. I had myself down as a blue person so I attached myself to the blue group. I felt strangely at home with my new group, really nice people, very chatty too. Mike had to ask us to keep a little quiet as he wanted to show us some more sales ideas. I looked around the room over to the red group. They all looked a little stern and serious and somewhat impatient to carry on. The yellow hubs were buzzing in the middle of the room, odd they chose the middle. And the greens were silent in the far corner. Louisa was with the green group and looked quite comfortable.

Mike then went around with his microphone and asked about each group, what we did and how we all sounded, so to show us how to recognise our customers' colour. I jotted down some notes.

Mike gave us all a handout, which I quickly stuck into my learning diary.

How to recognise customer's colours

	Around Them	What They Say	How They Talk	Body Language
Blue	• Photos • People Items	• Tells stories, anecdotes • Shares feelings • Informal speech • Expresses opinions • Digresses	• Lots of inflection • More pitch variation • Dramatic • High volume • Fast speech	• Animated expressions • Much hand/body movement • Contact oriented • Closeness • Spontaneous actions
Red	• Awards • Neat Piles • Power symbols • High backed chairs • Minimalism	• Tells more than asks • Talks more than listens • Emphatic statements • Blunt	• Forceful tone • Challenging tone • Loud, fast speech	• Firm handshake • Steady eye contact • Gestures to emphasise • Displays
Green	• Details • Systems charts • Organised • Functional	• Fact and task oriented • Limited sharing of feelings • More formal and proper • Focused	• Few pitch variations • Steady, monotone delivery • Slow, soft speech	• Few facial expressions • Non-contact oriented • Few gestures
Hub	• Teams • Membership symbols	• Questions to gather opinions • Inconsistent • Listen more than talks • Compromise language	• Variety of tone and expression • Lots of verbal nods	• Very open • Leaning forward • Non verbal nods • Mirrors body language naturally

Mike had us sit down as he began to explain how we could handle customers according to their colours. It was fascinating and as he spoke I began to recognise various customers from earlier in the week and how I treated them. I gulped when I realised where I was going wrong with people. I admitted to myself that I treated everyone like me, a blue, and handled them in the way I would like to be handled. And to some people that's not what they want. I jotted down how to handle each colour in my notepad and picked up the handout that Mike had given to everyone on how to influence and sell to each colour. What to do and what not to do.

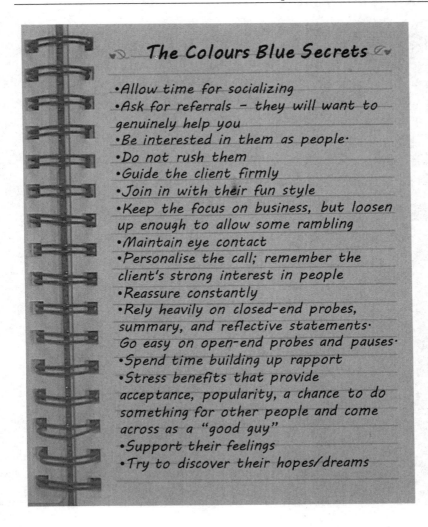

The Colours Blue Secrets

- Allow time for socializing
- Ask for referrals – they will want to genuinely help you
- Be interested in them as people.
- Do not rush them
- Guide the client firmly
- Join in with their fun style
- Keep the focus on business, but loosen up enough to allow some rambling
- Maintain eye contact
- Personalise the call; remember the client's strong interest in people
- Reassure constantly
- Rely heavily on closed-end probes, summary, and reflective statements. Go easy on open-end probes and pauses.
- Spend time building up rapport
- Stress benefits that provide acceptance, popularity, a chance to do something for other people and come across as a "good guy"
- Support their feelings
- Try to discover their hopes/dreams

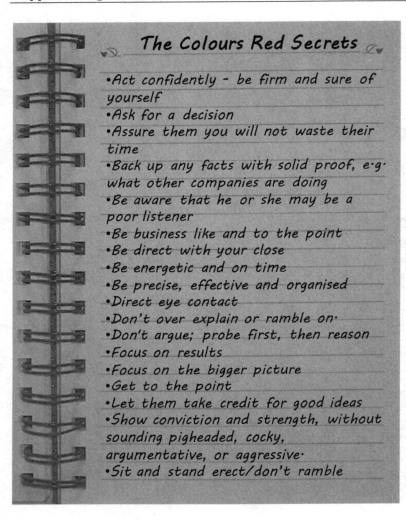

The Colours Red Secrets

- Act confidently - be firm and sure of yourself
- Ask for a decision
- Assure them you will not waste their time
- Back up any facts with solid proof, e·g· what other companies are doing
- Be aware that he or she may be a poor listener
- Be business like and to the point
- Be direct with your close
- Be energetic and on time
- Be precise, effective and organised
- Direct eye contact
- Don't over explain or ramble on·
- Don't argue; probe first, then reason
- Focus on results
- Focus on the bigger picture
- Get to the point
- Let them take credit for good ideas
- Show conviction and strength, without sounding pigheaded, cocky, argumentative, or aggressive·
- Sit and stand erect/don't ramble

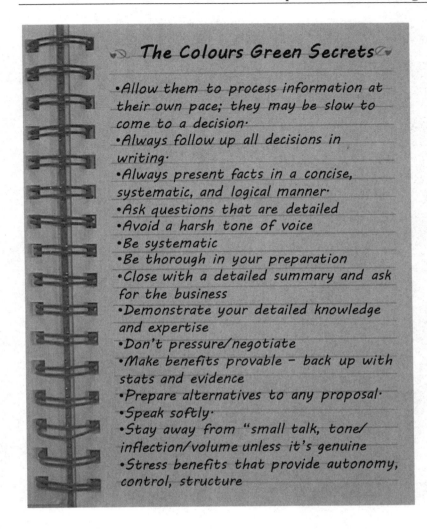

The Colours Green Secrets

- Allow them to process information at their own pace; they may be slow to come to a decision.
- Always follow up all decisions in writing.
- Always present facts in a concise, systematic, and logical manner.
- Ask questions that are detailed
- Avoid a harsh tone of voice
- Be systematic
- Be thorough in your preparation
- Close with a detailed summary and ask for the business
- Demonstrate your detailed knowledge and expertise
- Don't pressure/negotiate
- Make benefits provable – back up with stats and evidence
- Prepare alternatives to any proposal.
- Speak softly.
- Stay away from "small talk, tone/inflection/volume unless it's genuine
- Stress benefits that provide autonomy, control, structure

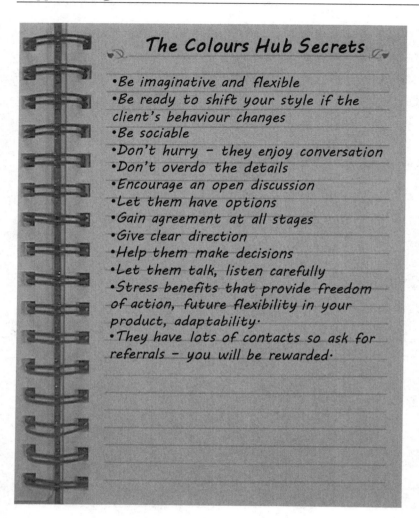

The Colours Hub Secrets

- Be imaginative and flexible
- Be ready to shift your style if the client's behaviour changes
- Be sociable
- Don't hurry – they enjoy conversation
- Don't overdo the details
- Encourage an open discussion
- Let them have options
- Gain agreement at all stages
- Give clear direction
- Help them make decisions
- Let them talk, listen carefully
- Stress benefits that provide freedom of action, future flexibility in your product, adaptability.
- They have lots of contacts so ask for referrals – you will be rewarded.

James, Louisa and I grabbed a quick drink after the meeting had finished. Louisa mentioned that she first encountered the colours a few years ago and used it all the time.

"So Doug, who do you know in your office and what colour are they?" asked Louisa.

"Uhmmm…." I thought. "I know what Keith is, he's a red through and through. Speaks his mind, gets to the point, knows what he wants, doesn't suffer fools, he's pacey, energetic and is success oriented."

"I'd agree with that," said James.

"Chloe… I'd put her down to be a yellow hub." Both agreed with that one.

"Vince, well he's a blue like me. I like Vince."

"People tend to gravitate towards their own colours. People like to deal with people who are like themselves," added Louisa.

"My mate, Jeff, is blue like me, as well, so that proves your theory. And you, Louisa, you're a green aren't you?"

"Yes, but with tinges of blue as well. And I think, Doug, that you have some green in you, as well. You seem to be driven by process and procedure, you're happy with the detail, you seem to want to improve, are quite happy to work on your own and operate independently."

"Wow, Louisa. You have a handle on me. I'd like to know more about this colour model." I said.

As we left the pub, I leaned over to Louisa. "Can you tell me more about the colours and I'll buy you dinner?"

"That'll be lovely, Doug. Shall we say Friday night?" she whispered as she drifted towards the tube station. That was a double result for the night as I walked in the opposite direction to catch the 73 bus back to my flat.

"So, how was the meeting last night, Doug?" called Keith.

"Excellent Keith, I learned about a model called the colours so you can handle people differently and sell to them in various ways to suit their values and drivers," I explained.

"You'll have to tell me more, Doug."

"OK Keith. I'll grab my coffee and be in your office." I paused, and then thought that Keith was red, so how would it be best for me to explain? Quick and to the point. Also, Mike said at the meeting that red people like quick information and the best way is to use a graphic or picture.

I dragged the flipchart into the room; Keith looked alarmed.

"Don't worry, Keith. I want to show the model to you in visual form."

"Go on then, Doug."

And within 5 minutes, Keith had a complete understanding.

"That was a really good description, Doug. Well done. But tell me, would you have done it like that if you hadn't known about my colour -- because I'm obviously a red?"

"No, Keith, if I'm honest…did it work for you?"

"Yes, it was right up my street. But do me favour, Doug, keep off the weasel words."

"What on earth is a weasel word?"

"A weasel word, Doug, is a filler -- a damp squid of a word which serves no purpose, such as absolutely, fundamentally, to be honest, obviously – they just annoy."

"Good spot, Keith."

"And whilst we're in the mood for some self-development, do you know why I'm a visual person?"

"Not really, Keith. I guess you just like to see things in pictures as they get a lot of information over in a quick timescale."

"That's right. There's 3 ways your customers like to think and have information given to them; visually, auditory and in a kinaesthetic manner."

"What does that mean, Keith?"

"Well it means that everyone can communicate in those three ways and has the thoughts in their head represented by these three ways. Visual is pictures, images, colour in the mind. Auditory is sounds, words, language, music in the mind and kinaesthetic is touch, feelings, tactile experiences. We all have a mixture, but most of us have a preference to communicate in one style. Mine is visual and most of the customers we see are the same."

"That's interesting Keith. I get a lot of hunches and gut feelings, but I do like to listen to people talk, conversation."

"And you talk a lot yourself, Doug. You're probably auditory in your preference and the problem most salespeople do is they communicate in their preferred style; like you, even if the customer is not the same as you."

"So if I waffle on to a visual person who's also a red, then I'm on a hiding to nothing?"

"That's right, Doug, unfortunately."

"So how should I recognise their preferred style, Keith?"

"The best way I've found is to watch their eyes. Let me show you on the flipchart, Doug."

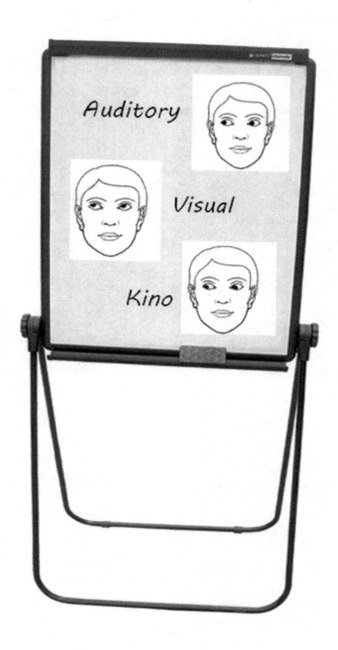

"So if someone keeps looking upwards, they're probably visual and I should communicate to them in a more visual way -- using diagrams, pictures, brochures. And if someone keeps glancing to their left or right, then they prefer to think in sounds, words, rhythm. And for those people who prefer to listen to me, I should slow down, talk to them carefully, take care with my words and sentences."

"That's right, Doug. And if someone looks downwards to their right…?"

"Then they're thinking in a kinaesthetic or kino manner and I ought to slow down, get them involved, feel the brochures, get reactions, ask how they are feeling about it?"

"That's the sum of it, Doug."

The morning was really busy, a typical Friday. I grabbed a sandwich for lunch and some coke and then settled down for some phone calls straight after lunch. I hadn't lost the habit of prospecting that Melanie taught me a few months ago. I try to make prospecting calls every day if I can.

Half way through my calls, Chloe walked into the office. I wasn't expecting her. She looked a little harassed and went straight in to talk to Keith. I could see them through Keith's glass door. He looked a little worried, too. I wondered what they were talking about.

Vince and I looked at each other. We were sensing something was up, but had no idea what it was.

"Fancy some tea, boys?" called Chloe as she stepped out of Keith's office.

"Not for me, thanks, Chloe. I'm off to see a new house in 5 minutes"

"I've just had one thanks, Chloe" I called back.

"Do you mind if I sit down, Doug?" asked Chloe.

"Not at all. How're things?" I asked.

"All good thanks, Doug… What have you got on this afternoon?"

I thought 'a suit and tie', but that was a little facetious and I sensed Chloe wasn't in the mood. "No appointments. I was going to clear up some paperwork and do some admin and some calls."

"Louisa tells me you enjoyed the colours presentation this week?"

"Yep, I did a lot. It's had a real impact on me and Keith told me about the VKA earlier, as well… visual, kinaesthetic and auditory."

"And how's it going to change the way you handle people, Doug?"

"Lots of ways. I've already been watching your eyes, Chloe," I blushed. "Not in that way. Sorry."

She looked down, "That's ok, Doug. I know you didn't mean that."

"There you go again. You look down to your right a lot."

"And..."

"Well that probably means you prefer to communicate in a kino manner -- preferring to get a feel for the conversation, understand fully and get involved if I were selling to you, Chloe -- knowing you're also blue. Am I right?"

"Yes Doug, you are."

"Then I'd take more time, check regularly how you're feeling about the meetings, get your views and opinions, get you talking a lot. I'd spend time building a rapport with you, maybe find out a little more about you, without being personal."

"Excellent Doug, this has made an impression, hasn't it?"

"Yes."

"I had an interesting visit to the South West region this week and picked up a really clever sales tactic from a number of their very successful advisers. They call it Package Selling. Are you interested in hearing a little more, Doug?"

"Yes, please."

"Notice I've picked up your eye movements and knowing you're an auditory person, you would like to hear about it, wouldn't you."

Chloe was a match for any sales adviser -- very quick and intelligent, but not arrogant with it.

"I overheard that, Chloe," Said Keith. "Do you mind if I listen in?"

"Of course not, Keith. Take a seat. The whole Package selling thing has turned on its head and their policy sales and customer feedback is at the highest it has ever been."

Keith and I looked fully sold on the evidence.

"Doug, let's say you've done your homework and you've arranged a mortgage, some life insurance, some health cover and a buildings policy for your customer and they're sitting in front of you in the office and you want them to snap it all up. How would you approach it?"

"I'd tell them how excited I am and how much work I've done on their case." I thought some more because I had to impress Chloe and Keith. "I'd then use the feature/benefit method they showed us at Central Training. This mortgage has a fixed rate which means you'll never have to worry about interest rates climbing and not being able to afford the loan," I boasted.

"That's good, Doug, and features/benefits selling really works. No one wants to hear features, but the world has moved on from benefit selling. The main thing I learned from the guys in the South West region is that customers can get all this from the internet and can find out about features and benefits from there. No, we need to be one step ahead and bring value to the process"

"So how can we do that, Chloe?"

"We need to get under the customer's skin more, and personalise a complete package to suit their needs, hence the term Package Selling. You do it in three stages, Doug. Stage one is to set out your stall and mention that you're going to tailor something that's going to suit them and be totally original and will take a lot of effort on your part, but we're really keen to ensure our mortgage package fits them like a glove. You want to pre-empt any problems that might occur so they don't head off to the internet because they will, Doug. More and more of your customers are buying the plans direct."

"I know. I do lose cases that way. What's the second stage, Chloe?"

"Stage 2 is to get to know their situation and the issues and problems they might face buying the home with a mortgage. You know... dying, illness and such. And stage 3 is presenting the whole package as one item -- not a collection of policies and plans. That's the key, Doug. They call it the 2fer1."

"The what?"

"The 2fer1. It means that for each sale or presentation to a customer, you're selling more than one plan, that's why it's called a package. You put in the same effort for more than one sale. Good, eh? And the best news is, we're giving the customer absolutely what they need and want and can afford."

I spotted the weasel word there, but didn't want to stop Chloe. She was on fire with this Package Selling concept and I must admit, so was I. Urrgg... another weasel word.

"Let me demonstrate, Doug."

"OK."

"So, Mr. and Mrs. Brown, I'm really pleased with what we've come up with for you. I've been researching all morning and liaising with colleagues, partners and systems to create a personalised mortgage package that, I think, fits you like a glove."

"Hey, clever stuff, Chloe," interrupted Keith, "you're making the invisible visible, aren't you."

"What's that, Keith?"

Keith had been holding his tongue up until now, but saw the opportunity to impress -- typical Keith. "When you sell a service -- something you can't touch like our agency service or Doug's advising -- then you have to impress on the customer what you do behind the scenes, so they know the effort you put in and can apply a value to the effort. It's called making the invisible visible"

"Nice one Keith, but Chloe, keep going." I took control. This was for my benefit.

"So, Mr. and Mrs. Brown, I'm really pleased with what we've come up with for you. I've been researching all morning and liaising with colleagues, partners and systems to create a personalised mortgage package that, I think, fits you like a glove." She repeated, "This personalised plan ensures you can buy the home you have in mind with a mortgage that's fixed for 5 years so you never need to worry about rates going sky high and not being able to afford the loan. The plan also makes sure that if either you or Mr. Brown were to die, the loan gets fully paid off. Also, if Mr. Brown is ill for longer than 3 months, we'll pick up the mortgage payments so you don't need to rush back to work before you're ready and, Mrs. Brown, you can carry on looking after the family. What's more, if your home burns down or gets destroyed in any way, we'll re-build it for you. How does that sound?"

"Hey, Chloe, that's really smooth. I like that. It's all one thing, one package -- not a series of bits to accept or decline on an individual basis."

"And I've left the best to last, Doug... Mr. and Mrs. Brown, you'll be pleased to know that I've arranged all of this for you within your maximum budget of £750 per month. In fact, it's come in at £723 in total. Shall we go into the detail and get the online submission done because I can take care of everything for you right now."

"Nice close at the end there, Chloe," impressed Keith.

"So your turn now, Doug. You present a package to me."

And I did with a round of applause from Keith, as well. I noted down the key points in my diary pretty much immediately as I didn't want to forget this one.

Package Selling

- Step 1 – set out your stall so customer knows you do personal packages
- Step 2 – get to know their situation and problems
- Step 3 – 2fer1 – presenting the whole package
- Making visible what's invisible

Chloe's Presentation Script

So Mr and Mrs Brown I'm really pleased with what we've come up with for you. I've been researching all morning and liaising with colleagues, partners and systems to create a personalised mortgage package that, I think, fits you like a glove." She repeated, "This personalised plan ensures you can buy the home you have in mind with a mortgage that's fixed for 5 years so you never need to worry about rates going sky high and not being able to afford the loan.

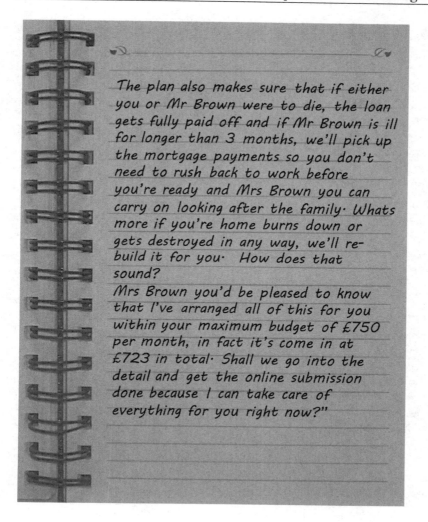

The plan also makes sure that if either you or Mr Brown were to die, the loan gets fully paid off and if Mr Brown is ill for longer than 3 months, we'll pick up the mortgage payments so you don't need to rush back to work before you're ready and Mrs Brown you can carry on looking after the family. Whats more if you're home burns down or gets destroyed in any way, we'll rebuild it for you. How does that sound?

Mrs Brown you'd be pleased to know that I've arranged all of this for you within your maximum budget of £750 per month, in fact it's come in at £723 in total. Shall we go into the detail and get the online submission done because I can take care of everything for you right now?"

We closed up at 5pm that night; we always close on time on a Friday.

I needed to pop into PC World to pick up my laptop. They were willing to reformat the hard-drive and load Windows 7 for me at a reasonable price as I didn't know how to do it nor did I have the time. I walked into the store and went over to the TechGuys section. At the counter, the man went over to get my laptop. Through the Perspex glass behind him, I could clearly see three TechGuys and one TechGirl fixing computers, heads in PC Cases, screens of diagnostics scrolling down at a rapid pace, screwdrivers unclipping delicate hard-drives, and beads of sweat dripping from the forehead of a technician carefully loading a graphics card.

Now I knew what Keith had said earlier. Making the invisible visible. The TechGuys clearly were showing the effort and complexity of the service they offered. They could've had a barrier and hidden the Techguys, but they preferred to show customers exactly what their service involved. Very clever.

On my way out, my phone rang. I could see it was Louisa.

"Hi Doug, how're things?"

"Great thanks, Louisa."

"So what's the plan tonight then, Doug?"

I thought for a moment. I'd booked a restaurant, but I thought about this package concept so continued, "Well Louisa, I've created a personalised evening for you tonight having thought long and hard as to what we can do. You're going to have a great evening and be able to relax, unwind, and enjoy my company. We're eating at Ronnie's at 8pm and I'll pick you up at 7.30. From there, I've got two tickets for the new George Clooney movie I know you're going to enjoy, and then maybe a nightcap before I take you home. How does that sound Louisa?"

"Fabulous, Doug. Chloe's been to see you as well, has she?"

I blushed, but it made Louisa smile. Even I could see that on the phone or hear it in her voice.

In the shower, I thought about the last few days and all the things I'd learned about people, characters, behaviours, colours and thinking styles. From now on, I'm never going to treat everyone the same.

Chapter 7 – I need to think about it

In which Doug learns how to read the signals and close the sale

Now I know what Keith and Chloe were talking about last week. Figures, numbers, targets. And mine weren't on stream. I was 3 months into the job and not on target and for a salesperson, that wasn't good news. Chloe and Keith had been examining and discussing why the numbers were down and Chloe had the answer.

"Talk to me, Doug."

"Blimey, it's a bit of a shock actually, Chloe. I kinda knew, but figured they weren't going to be that bad."

"Any ideas, Doug?"

Chloe was playing the coach's game, but I could see in her eyes she meant business.

"I'll keep at it, Chloe. I'll just carry on as I'm doing and I'm sure the business will come through. I'm seeing a lot of people, my diary is always full… I can't help it if they don't all go ahead," I continued defensively.

"OK Doug. I've got a plan and some ideas for you to get your numbers back up to speed for the next quarter and Keith is agreeing with me on this, as well."

"Go on, Chloe." I was open to suggestions.

"Doug, you're a nice guy. Mr. Nice Guy and you don't like rejection or people saying 'no' to you. You even got quite defensive with me a second ago."

"No, I don't." I realised what I just said.

"There you go, again. I've seen it before and the way it affects your results, Doug, is that you don't like asking for the business, closing, objection handling… all those things they taught you at Central Training. You don't like to do them because you don't want upset or rejection. So many of your clients to whom you've given really good advice, just do it themselves. On the internet or with other advisers, they do it themselves. Possibly that's the way they think it should be done.

So for the next few coaching sessions, we're going to take a look at how you steer the client to actually buy the mortgage and the insurances you've advised, Doug. How does that sound?"

"OK Chloe." My mind was wandering. That was a shell of feedback, but probably true.

The day dragged to an end. I was under a little pressure and I didn't like it. It made everything seem far more serious, and if I didn't get the numbers back up, I wouldn't be around for much longer and I really enjoyed this job.

It's got to be the right time for Steve, now. Chicago is 6 hours behind so it'll be about 5 o'clock over there. Yes, he's online, let's see if he's available.

Skype's a great piece of kit. I could see Steve quite vividly and hear him clearly. "Hi, Doug. How's it all going down there in that little country of yours?"

"Don't be cheeky, just 'cos you're in the States. Things going well. What about you Bro?"

"All good, Doug. Have you spoken to the folks recently?"

"No, I haven't, should though, feel a bit guilty. Anyway Steve, I wanted to ask you a question?"

"Go on, Bro."

"I'm under a bit of pressure at work -- started today. The boss needs me to close more business,"

"Mmmm, sounds like you are under some pressure, Doug, like you need some ideas. Do you use iTunes, Doug?"

"Yes, I do. I've got an iPod and use it to download music and podcasts."

"Search for closing techniques. Look out for a podcast from Dane Dale, he's a Brit and really good.

"Thanks, Steve. That's a great tip. I'll do it now"

"When it comes to objections, Doug, I always build in the answers before they become problems. It's called pre-empting the objection. Do you do that?"

"I don't think so"

"Google it, Doug. Pleasure to be of service, sir." Steve signed off in a very realistic American accent.

ITunes, Podcasts, let's log on there. Sales tips, closing tips… press send. Wow, there's loads of podcasts. Ah… here's one from Dane Dale. Let me click on that one.

An hour later and I was listening to the podcast on my iPhone. I'd downloaded the last 12 month's worth and I started to scroll through to find some on closing skills. "The real secret to overcoming objections." That's got my name on it.

"Hi, I'm Dane Dale and that's danedale.com. As a kid, I was fascinated when doctors would carefully tap a patient's knee with a small hammer and the patient's leg would involuntarily kick upwards. That's where the phrase "knee jerk reaction" comes from. For years after first seeing this on TV, I tried in vain to make my knee do the same with plenty of bruises to show for my efforts.

Life is full of knee jerk reactions. People get used to reacting in a certain way, especially when they are being offered to buy something. You see, when faced with a decision to buy something, we will revert to a knee jerk reaction and say something like, "No thanks" or "I'll think about it" or "Send/email me some brochures."

Unfortunately, many salespeople or those on the front line who need to sell things, accept these customer reactions and don't close on the sale.

And this is a shame because they are often not real reasons.

The secret is to accept them for what they are… knee jerk reactions and kind of ignore them and try again. Throw in a holding phrase and re-do your close. If done carefully and subtly, it won't harm and may get the customer to think it through again and make a positive decision.

Some favourite responses that won't offend…

"That's fine, I'm only asking for a short chat with our adviser -- it won't harm will it?"

"I understand, however the benefits are excellent…."

"Are you sure? You'll be missing out on…"

"I could email you some brochures, but I've a better idea. Let's meet shortly to talk it through…"

Bear in mind that a customer's first reaction to your close is normally a "no" because this is an in-built knee jerk reaction.

The second, more significant Knee Jerk Reaction comes from us, the salesperson. When a customer gives us an objection or reservation which might be entirely understandable and realistic, we immediately come in with a pre-thought through answer to the objection. Especially if we've just come back from a training course and we know all the answers to common objections.

Again the trick is to react differently. A nifty little reminder here is to imagine sitting on their lap. Of course, this is a metaphor and not something to actually do, although that depends on your customer, I guess. No, I'm saying we follow the LAP rule – L for listen to the reservation and really hear them out first. Then we A, acknowledge it. I'm not saying agree with them, but see their point of view. Understand where they're coming from. And the final, P, is to probe to figure out exactly what it is they have an issue with.

"I can see where you're coming from there and it's a fine point you're making... can I just ask... is that the only issue that might prevent you going ahead with this plan?"

This strategy gives you thinking time, ensures that your customer knows they're being listened to and shows you're on their side.

So consider the two knee jerk reactions the next time you're in a sales situation. The customer's reaction to your close and your potential quick response to their reservation. They are both hazardous in their own right.

And try as I may, I still can't get my knee to kick upwards every time I whack it with a hammer. Maybe if I hit it harder..."

Hey that Dale or Dane or Dean, he's a rule speaker dude. I liked the idea of knee jerk reactions and LAP. What was it again? I reached for my diary and at the same time, I Googled pre-empting objections.

I felt invigorated in the morning. A run in the park – now that it was getting lighter in the mornings, this made running so easy.

During my run, I figured out what I was going to do to pre-empt the objections that I typically get. I was going to talk about budgets right up front so I could fit a package to suit their needs, but also to fit their budget. Explain upfront how I work and that I'll ask them to go ahead with the paperwork if what I recommend suits them.

I'm also going to explain that I'm paid by the actual paperwork going ahead so the customer appreciates what they need to do. Ask them if they intend to see anyone else and really make sure they know why I'm unique.

My diary so far today, but I get the impression I'm going to be adding to this.

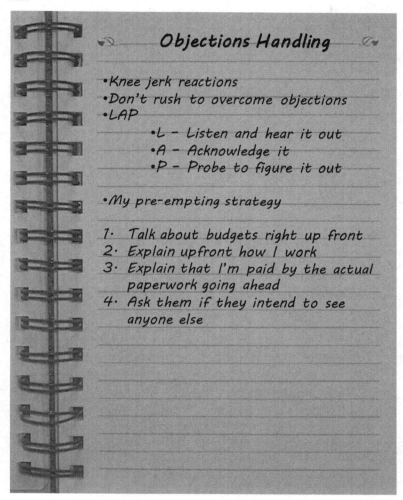

Objections Handling

- Knee jerk reactions
- Don't rush to overcome objections
- LAP
    - L – Listen and hear it out
    - A – Acknowledge it
    - P – Probe to figure it out

- My pre-empting strategy

1. Talk about budgets right up front
2. Explain upfront how I work
3. Explain that I'm paid by the actual paperwork going ahead
4. Ask them if they intend to see anyone else

The run was invigorating, just what I needed after a long night listening to podcasts. A quick shower, change and into the office. I was first in, too.

Second into the office was Vince, soon followed by Keith, rather later than normal and with a big beaming smile.

"Come on Keith, shouted Vince, who is she? You look like you're in love."

"None of your business, Vincenzo," Keith always addressed Vince in that way, but the two boys did get on well.

During the morning meeting, Keith explained that he had secured a lucrative new listing last night from Mr. and Mrs. Beddows, who said they were also interested in having a mortgage organised for them and he wanted me to pop along this morning with him.

Always a pleasure to jump into Keith's car, a nice set of wheels. And he was proud of it, too. Keith was in a particularly good mood today and you could tell he was feeling rather confident. At the traffic lights, he began.

"Doug, what do traffic lights tell you?"

"That's a bit obvious Keith. I can drive, you know."

"No, I'm being serious."

"OK, red means stop and wait because other traffic will be crossing, amber means proceed but with caution and green means go ahead at full speed."

"Exactly, Doug and that's what you want to imagine your customer is. I do. I put a traffic light above their head and see a colour. If I see green, it tells me that the customer likes what I'm saying and is happy for me to progress with the sales process. If I see amber, there's possibly something wrong but I continue, keeping a close eye on them."

"And red Keith?"

"Ah red. Danger. Something is wrong, I don't know what, so I need to ask what's happening. I might say – how does this feel to you? – or – is everything OK so far? – so I can gauge their reaction. But above all, I don't just carry on, regardless, because there's something up."

"That's quite clever Keith. I like that." Keith liked compliments. "But how do you know what colour they are?"

"Instinct and insight, Doug. I see it in their body language. I look for openness in their bodies such as open arms, hands on the desk, smiles, eye contact. These are all positive signs."

I chipped in, "and closed signs are crossed arms, crossed legs, looking away. That's what Allan Pease taught me."

"No that's rubbish actually, Doug. Some people are just that way inclined and you shouldn't read into one or two signals."

"So how do you read a red or amber?" I defended.

"By their leakage."

"Their what?" I didn't have the heart to say I'd heard about leakage from Allan Pease.

"Their leakage, Doug. Let me explain" and as we pulled away at the traffic lights, Keith let me into one of his trade secrets. "What I do is check their normal style, their normal posture, how they normally give me eye contact. And if they suddenly change in some way, such as looking away from me, or leaning back, crossing their arms, they've leaked their body language. They're showing me leakage which is normally saying something is wrong."

"That's excellent Keith, I'll remember that one. Are there any other ways to gauge their traffic light colour?"

"By what they say. Someone who is asking questions is very interested, particularly if they want to know about our fee or when we can start marketing; that's a great signal. Also if they turn to their partner and whisper a question or two that might indicate amber. If they go all silent on me, that's usually red."

"I'll look out for that Keith, thanks."

"Hold the thanks, Doug. We've arrived at the Beddows place. What do you think?"

"Nice pad, Keith, and a private drive as well."

"First impressions Doug -- so important when selling a house and for any salesperson, as well. When they greet us at the door, they'll take…"

"90 seconds to form a lasting impression." I added.

"Exactly Doug. Glad you're learning something."

Two hours later, we were steaming down the Tottenham High Road back to the office. "Nice close that Keith, the way you recognised the green light and you whipped out the sales contract for them to sign and you even had your pen ready, as well."

"Yes, it was good wasn't it," boasted Keith, as of course he often did. But recognition due, he secured the listing and an appointment for me to speak to the Beddows on Friday morning to organise their mortgage.

"So what's the big grin about Keith?"

"And so you may ask. Her names' Sue. Met her a couple of days ago; I think it's serious."

"Good news, Keith. Will she make an honest man of you?"

"Not sure about that. Hey, we're out this Friday. We're going to Mondells in the High Road. Vincenzo's coming with his girlfriend. Aren't you seeing Louisa from Hackney branch?"

"How did you know, Keith?"

"Keith knows everything" he smiled "Fancy coming?"

"Sounds fun, I'll text Louisa now"

"Lou x fancy clubbing Mondells Friday night, boys and Bffs coming.x."

Almost instantly a return.

"Luv to Doug - missin you xx."

That's a nice text back from Louisa, 2 kisses. I am doing well. But, to matters in hand. I need to start closing business and tonight I have a potential piece of business. I'm going to use the traffic lights and pre-empting with the customers.

I locked the door after they'd gone. It was a late appointment and I was the only one left in the office, or so I thought.

"How'd it go, Dougy" called out Keith.

"I didn't see you there, Keith."

"I'm just out, date with the lovely Sue. I'm taking her to the new Vietnamese restaurant down Lordship Lane, mustn't be late. so how'd it go... the Hendersons?"

"They said they want to think about it and they'll come back to me tomorrow."

"Doug, Doug, Doug...you're missing a trick. Anyway, I gotta dash. See you tomorrow."

"Night Keith." What did he mean by I'm missing a trick? I pre-empted things and read their traffic light colours perfectly, I thought. I'm gonna listen to more podcasts tonight. I need to crack this.

An omelette beautifully cooked, I thought, and a can of beer and onto the iPod to listen to Dane Dale's podcast entitled – gaining commitment and closing – exactly what I was looking for. Diary at hand to make notes.

"Hi. Dane Dale here, that's danedale.com. Let me talk to you about gaining commitment from customers.

As soon as the New Year starts, my wife will always make her homemade turkey soup. The turkey carcass boils on the stove all day. Her turkey soup is legendary because it feeds my whole family for days on end and is absolutely delicious.

We eat it for lunch, for tea and even in flasks when we enjoy our New Year walks. It's kind of a ritual to bring in the new year.

Good grief, just writing this is making me hungry.

Eating the soup is like closing sales. There's no way I'd ever dive into the soup, take an enormous spoonful and gulp it down. I'd scoop up a little, blow on it, feel the steam with my top lip, take a sip and only then would I take a decent mouthful.

Closing the sale is the same concept. You wouldn't go charging in would you?

Five minutes into the sale would you say, "Would you like to sign the paperwork now, Mrs. Brown?"

You'd end up with a handbag around your chops!

No, you'd wait until Mrs. Brown was ready to buy your product or service and only then would you ask. You have a much better chance of getting a 'yes' rather than a refusal. And nobody likes to be refused, which is another reason why plenty of sales people don't ever ask for the sale… they don't like to be rejected.

If you test the soup first to see how hot it is, you'll not burn your tongue. Likewise, if you test the customer first, you'll not spoil the deal. So how do you do this?

It's like dating in your early teens. Before you asked the person out for the date of their dreams, you checked with their friends to see if they were seeing anyone else and you might even have spoken to their best friends to assess your chances. Only then did you pluck up enough courage to ask them out.

People that didn't follow this rule were either really successful in the dating stakes or had red cheeks from all those slaps!

Now I do know of salespeople who are like this. They are so hardened to rejection, that they don't really care anymore and just ask everyone. The double glazing, cold calling merchants are like this. You say 'no' so they go onto the next customer…eventually someone is going to say yes.

But I don't like to teach selling that way... I like to enjoy my job and the rapport we build with customers. It's all about asking questions...

The three types of questions you will want to ask leading up to the close are testing questions to feel the temperature of the soup, trial questions to taste a little of the soup and then closing questions to drink the soup. Testing questions first:

"How do you feel about those benefits?"

"They sound good?"

"Does it all make sense so far?"

"Yes thank you"

"Have I missed anything you'd like to know about?"

"No? Everything's been covered?"

Trial Questions next.

Back to my dating analogy... I remember when I met my wife at a party for the first time. Obviously, she wasn't my wife then! "Jo," I said, getting terribly tongue tied, "hypothetically speaking, if I was to take you out one evening, would you have any objections?" She accused me of being a lawyer at that moment and I nearly blew it completely. Twenty years later, we now laugh about my ridiculous trial close. Although not very elegant, it worked. It made her laugh and she said she would say 'yes'. So I did and here I am today, happily married and with three children, too.

The same process needs to be followed in sales. You've tested the water and now need to be sure the customer is ready to say 'yes'.

Questions are needed here which serve as trial closes. A few questions need asking such as:

"Is this what you had in mind?"

"Does this fit your budget?"

"If I can arrange that for you, would you be interested?"

"Are you OK with the whole package?"

In many cases, your questions will throw up "no's" or "I'm not sure" or "I'll let you know". Dealing with customer concerns deserves more time spent, which I'll give you later. But the best learning point here is that customer concerns or issues tell you how close you are to the final close. If you have too many concerns from your customer, they're not ready to buy so you'll want to go back to more benefits or re-analysing their real needs. Get yourself into reverse gear.

Non verbal trial closing is great fun. My favourite is to place the contract or application form or whatever needs signing in the middle of the table for them to take. A sure sign they want to go ahead.

The other non verbal trial close is silence but you need to combine this with a question. For example:

"If we got this going for you, would you be interested in going ahead right now?"

Closing Questions next, folks.

When I've tested the temperature of my wife's soup and taken a sip, I then have no hesitation in taking a really big spoonful and popping this straight into my mouth. Mmm…this tastes really good. I just know it's going to be delicious."

In the same way, if you've tested the customer for a buying signal and trialled some questions with them, then you just know they're going to say 'yes'. You just expect or assume they'll buy.

So phrase your closing questions assuming they'll say 'yes'.

"Let's go ahead, then?"

"Shall we fill in the forms straightway then?"

"Shall we get the ball rolling then?"

"Would you like me to fill in the application form for you now?"

"How would you like to pay?"

Remember to go silent just after you've asked the final close question. Look at them, smile and wait. Easier said than done I know. Silence can be very loud in these situations, but you need to keep quiet."

I did enjoy that podcast Dane, I can see a hot bowl of soup. Must remember to test close, trial close, then ask. That's pretty easy. Let me note that down. His next podcast is called *Closing Techniques*, like this one. So I took another large swig of beer, laid back on the couch and began.

"Hi. Dane Dale here. That's danedale.com. Let me talk to you about closing and my 3-Part Convincers; they're so cool.

The magic of this hypnotic closing skill is the rhythm of three -- sometimes called triples. The fact is, that everything comes in threes. Three is a magic number and falls off the tongue smoothly and effortlessly.

The tip here is to give only three benefits or three reasons or three advantages -- ever.

And when closing, you could use the 3-part convincer, which is a set of three statements. These statements are, without doubt, true and most people will find themselves in agreement.

They are a great calming skill and all you're doing here is confirming to the customer what is true in their minds and allowing them to go into a state of comfort where there are no hidden surprises.

Simply say things that are true for the customer. Keep them global at first such as...

"It's a beautiful day today, isn't it?"

"Parking's a bit tricky in town at this time."

Then later on you could use some truisms you've found out about the customer such as...

"Your family is a real priority to you, aren't they?"

"From the information on the form, you obviously keep yourselves fit and healthy."

"Getting a service that will save you time is important to you, don't you think?"

As the customer relaxes and sees that your product is right for them... introduce some specific truisms, such as...

"So you agree your budget for the package is just under £600 per month?"

"You'd like to complete the forms now?"

Notice that I've tagged some of the questions at the end with what we call a 'yes tag'. So let me talk to you about yes tags, They're the best.

These are little words at the end of the statements to get a positive 'yes' from the customer -- useful for gaining commitment to move the sale along. Yes tags come in all sorts of shapes and sizes and I just know you've used them before without knowing what they were called... haven't you?

Examples of yes tags are 'haven't you', 'aren't you', 'don't you', 'isn't it' and 'won't you'.

Just put one at the end of a truism statement and your customer will want to nod their head in agreement.

But I'm sure you'll agree, won't you, that overuse is dangerous. Chocolate is lovely in small doses - too much and you can become very queasy, indeed..."

...don't you think? As I laid down on my pillow, I thought back to the Hendersons and tried to figure out what I could've done differently. And then it came to me. If I had tested them a little earlier and used a trial close half way through the meeting, I would've been able to see how they felt at the time. Obviously, I hadn't covered something or I'd confused them or they weren't really interested in using me. Had I realized this earlier, I could've done something about it. Easy, really -- when you think about it.

Friday arrived.

"Mr. and Mrs. Beddows, can I take it that you'll be happy for me to organise your mortgage package for you when you sell Four Winds and find a house to buy?"

"You have my word, young man."

And later in the afternoon...

"How's it all sounding to you, Mike?"

"So Mike, this is exactly what you're looking for, isn't it?"

"Shall we go ahead right away?"

"Yes, Doug, let's do it now, thanks."

It was all coming together. This week alone I've put away three deals worth over £5,000. I'm going to phone Chloe.

"That's fabulous news, Doug, well done. I'm thrilled for you. I guess you're going to have a good night at the club tonight. Fantastic."

"How did you know I was going clubbing Chloe?"

"Louisa told me in confidence, Doug. She seems to quite like you. Have a great time tonight. Oh, I wanted to mention it in case you speak with Vicky. Awful news. Her partner has been officially declared KIA."

"KIA?"

"Killed in Action. She's off at the moment. In case you speak to her, thought I'd better let you know... in case."

"Night, Chloe."

Gosh, poor Vicky. I wondered about calling her, but wasn't sure whether I should. Poor thing, how terrible.

I didn't.

"How are you, Doug?" as Louisa leaned across to kiss me before buckling up in her seat belt.

"I'm good Lou, thanks. Looking forward to letting my hair down a little tonight. What about you?"

"I just love dancing -- been looking forward all week. Have you met the boys' girlfriends? I wonder what they're like."

"Dunno, never met them before. They'll be fun."

"I've missed you this week, Doug."

"That's great, Lou."

Louisa went quiet on me. Had I said something wrong? But the club beckoned and I needed to find somewhere to park.

Inside the club we found a snug place to sit, Keith got the drinks in and introduced us to Sue. Vince had not yet arrived.

"Sue seems nice," shouted Louisa into my ear, as this was the only way to hear each other. "This is a nice place, Doug, Thanks for taking me. Are you having a nice time?"

"Yes, it's great."

Later, on the dance floor "It's lovely being with you Doug; are you enjoying yourself?"

Later "Can we do this again, Doug?"

And later as I dropped her off at her home "Are we seeing each other tomorrow night, Doug?"

"Uhmmmm, I'm out with my mate, Jeff, tomorrow Louisa. Sorry"

"Oh that's alright, Doug. Perhaps Sunday?"

"I'm not sure what I'm doing Sunday, Louisa. I think I'm due to visit my neighbours for Sunday dinner."

"Ok, shame..."

"Let me text you tomorrow then, Louisa," I lied, having survived the onslaught intact. Talk about gaining commitment and closing techniques -- Louisa was a master.

"Jeff" it was just too much. What should I do mate?"

"Did you text her about tomorrow?"

"No."

"Well don't."

"Good advice, Jeff," as I potted the black ball to win the first frame. A good week all round.

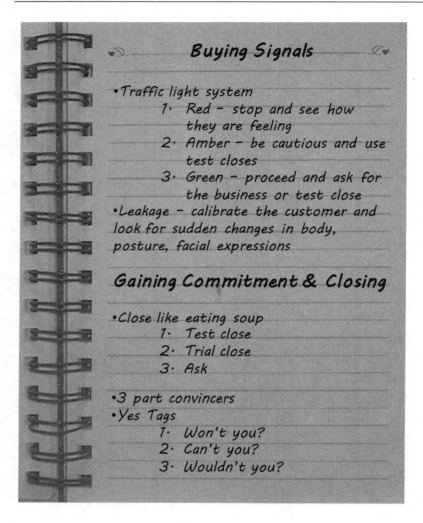

Buying Signals

- Traffic light system
    1. Red – stop and see how they are feeling
    2. Amber – be cautious and use test closes
    3. Green – proceed and ask for the business or test close
- Leakage – calibrate the customer and look for sudden changes in body, posture, facial expressions

Gaining Commitment & Closing

- Close like eating soup
    1. Test close
    2. Trial close
    3. Ask

- 3 part convincers
- Yes Tags
    1. Won't you?
    2. Can't you?
    3. Wouldn't you?

Chapter 8 – Not another cancellation

In which Doug discovers the secret of self discovery and emotional selling

Monday was terrifically busy. I had appointments back to back. I must stop calling them appointments, that's what you have at the dentists. Tuesday was just as busy and both days I wrote 3 cases -- with insurance as well. The agency secured deals on 5 properties, including Mr. and Mrs. Beddows' High Acres and they were thrilled (as was I) when I organised their mortgage at the weekend. The biggest case I'd ever arranged and worth a huge amount to the branch.

All was going well. I'd even gotten my running up to 2 hours in the park and on the treadmill in the gym. The only sour note was Louisa's text.

So you not going to call then, Doug?

Jeff's strategy I stuck to and I hadn't -- hadn't called.

In the end, I knew I had to call and explain. "I'm not ready for commitment, Louisa. Sorry, it's not you -- it's me," just didn't cut it, but it's all I could think of saying. Better keep away from Hackney branch for a few weeks.

After lunch was my time for emails. I liked to clear my inbox three times a day rather than every minute, which some of the advisers did. 9am, 2pm and 5pm were email times and I began to trawl through the emails. Here's one from Head Office Cancellations. It was an automated email:

> "Three client cancellations received in month so far, exception report generated to sales manager."

Gulp, that's not good. Chloe will be on my back with that one. The cancellations were all policies I sold the previous month, which went into force immediately. All that work for nothing as the clients had simply cancelled the policies with head office. To say I was annoyed was an understatement. I was furious!

But, at least, Chloe kept her cool. "Why do you think, Doug?"

"I don't know, Chloe. I really don't know. They needed the plan and my advice was spot on. I just can't understand why... they could afford it."

"Doug, how are you getting on with the Package Selling idea I told you about the other week?"

"OK I guess; it's not as easy as it appears when you showed me and demonstrated."

"I'm convinced that if you were to master that, then these cancellations wouldn't happen, so…"

"You sound pretty convinced Chloe."

"I phoned the customers -- a bit of customer satisfaction research, and they all told me that once they received the paperwork and the direct debit, they couldn't recall why they bought it. They couldn't see the benefit -- the value."

"So what next, Chloe?"

"A residential course at head office. One of the guys from the South West region has been seconded to the training department and is running Package Selling courses to the whole network and I've scheduled you. You'll get an email later today from training and you'll be mixing with others from the country, so you can pick up some best practice ideas to bring back with you. Listen Doug, this is important. You need to crack this cancellation thing; otherwise, it'll undo all the good work that you've been achieving recently. You look as if you've turned the corner with business. Keith's dead chuffed with you."

"Is he? He never said."

"He told me earlier that he really likes you in the office. You're an asset to the whole team and a breath of fresh air and a big profit contributor too."

"I wished he'd tell me that, but at least I know. Thanks Chloe, you're the best."

The rest of the day, I mulled over the cancellations. I had a meeting with a customer in the afternoon and I probably overdid the value bit of the plans I was selling. It just never seems to get there; I just never seem to crack it. I wonder if I will. Self doubt creeping in again, and I was having a conversation with myself about it.

No email from head office, but my mind turned to my Marathon planning. My running had improved and I was trying to do two hours at a time. I was up to about 15Ks but had to step up somewhat. I had never run 26 miles before. The added pressure was that I was getting sponsorship money since I opened the Virgin Charity site and created my own page. Put it out on Facebook and my friends were all donating money. So I have to do it. And only a couple of months to go. I'd better get cracking. The gym was no good since you're time limited on the treadmill when it's busy. I needed some inspiration.

I found it on the running forum. A great place to chat with other people about running. I asked the question, a very small but loud – help. Instantly the replies came back -- some really good ideas. Vary your sport, do some swimming, weights, endurance, get a coach, just run, catch a train to a far spot and run home. Brilliant. I liked the idea from a guy called Fred from Taunton who was running in the same marathon as me. He suggested increasing my duration by a kilometre a week until I reached my target. He mentioned that a little and often is the way to increase your distance but don't run every day. Have a day's rest in between.

A final tip amazed me. He said not to listen to music whilst running. Instead, listen to your body. Imagine you are the controller, he said, and check with your legs, your knees, your ankles, your heart constantly to see how they doing.

That night, with the long evenings available I managed 16K which took me hour and half without my MP3. I'm on it, Techtronic.

Reading through the email from head office training, to see who I knew. Don't know, heard of, never heard, heard of...Vicky...how wonderful to see Vicky again.

A quick text.

"Hi Vicky. Doug here, c u on course next month."

Ten seconds later...

"Doug, see spl not getting better, should be good. V."

I replied...

"How u getting there?"

Ten seconds later...

"On train, changing in London arriving at Victoria Station."

I responded...

"I'm driving up, can I pick u up Victoria Station and drive you?"

Five seconds later

"Lush Doug, thx."

And the rest of the day went really well. I felt good inside – excited -- not sure why. Looking forward to the course, my running, my job was going really well... must speak to Mum and Dad though. But, then a text came through from Jeff.

"Uncle Jeff here calling Uncle Doug for beer at Snooker Club tonight, pls respond."

"C U tonite Jeff, usual time."

I think texts are one of the best inventions ever.

The station pick up allowed for a maximum of 25 minutes and the security guys looked menacing. Where was she? I got out of the car and entered the station. Victoria station is a magnificent building. As a country, we have so benefited from the Victorian spending on railway infrastructure in the 19th century. It was a beautiful day for driving, clear blue skies and about 21 degrees. I had downloaded a decent Sat Nav programme for my iPhone, Co Pilot 9, already primed with the directions.

We were training in an old country mansion which had been converted to a conference centre a few years' ago. I'd already Googled Earthed it and worked out a running track for the evenings. We were staying over tonight and tomorrow night, as well.

There she is. Casual. Jeans and sweatshirt.

"Hi Vicky, you Ok?"

"Hi Doug, little delay. I'm sorry."

"Let me take that for you."

I heaved her case into the boot. How long were we staying over? Two nights? She seemed to have enough for a fortnight.

We sped out of London on the A1, onto the M25 and turned off at the A10. The Sat Nav worked a treat and let me concentrate on talking to Vicky. As we cruised along the A10 and the Sat Nav said 30 minutes to go, I felt relaxed and comfortable. Vicky wasn't very chatty; I didn't like to ask.

"I'm so sorry what happened, Vicky"

"Thank you Doug, and thanks for asking. It's been terrible I must admit but I'm moving forward."

I've always been unsure in such situations and after some nervous silence, I turned to a man's answer and started talking about work.

"So we haven't seen each other since the first training course back in January. How's your business doing? I see your name up at the top of tables for the South region."

"It's going well Doug, thanks. What about you?"

"OK… hey Vicky let's play a game for the remainder of the journey.

"OK."

"You share me two things that have worked for you and I'll do the same."

"Alright Doug, that sounds useful. Who starts?"

"I'll start with one idea."

So I did. I shared with her the traffic light technique Allan and Keith had shown me.

"I like that, Doug. That's really visual and you know I'm very visual. OK, my turn. I use two types of questions, and they're not open and closed."

I laughed.

"I use towards and away from questions with my clients when I'm disturbing them to need protection. I'll start with towards type questions as I want to find out what my client is aiming towards in their life. Is it a house by the sea, a comfy retirement, private schooling for little Jonny…? Later on, I link the benefits from the various protection plans to help them afford these things if anything happens to either of them."

"That's clever, Vicky, and what are away from questions?"

"Those are the opposite. Do you remember the embarrassment of BP and the Gulf Oil slick and the terrible human tragedy that unfolded, Doug?"

"Yes I do. That was awful for the people living along the coastline."

"The chances of this event happening were very low but, the impact was enormous, affecting thousands of people. I read recently that a plug, or technically put, an acoustic shut off switch, could've been bought and installed for $500,000 but was deemed too expensive at the time. Seems like a bargain now.

Likewise, the impact of having a serious illness or dying is just as catastrophic for our clients, but the chances of this event happening is also low. Our job is to help our clients see the shattering consequences for them.

How do we do this, Doug?"

"We tell them of course, Vicky. Even I know that one."

"We can, yes, but it's more powerful if they discover it themselves. It's the same as telling an alcoholic they're drinking too much, but the result will be in one ear and out the other. No, the secret is self-discovery. They have to figure it out themselves. We're not preachers."

"So how do we do that?"

I've got some ideas. Ask yourself what problems do our products solve? For example, if you have Permanent Health Insurance, the problems are having no money to pay the bills and having to rush back to work before you're ready. Suggest the problem to your client, and then ask how the problem will affect them.

Come out with the difficult questions. Have some rescue questions available that just get to the point. "Tell me Brian, if you were to be off ill from work for a long time, how would you cope with all the bills?" Remember to let your client figure it all out, don't fill in the gaps for them.

Ask them what might happen if... death, illness, house fire... and then just give them a stare. Let them think it through, see the implications, the disaster for their family, the repercussions. Only when they can really see it, visualise it, feel it themselves, know what it's like to drive around in a wheelchair...will they realise they need some protection.

The secret Doug, is not say too much. Listen, nod, probe a little, ask them to expand on that, to tell you more. Use assertions, such as 'really,' 'gosh,' sound genuinely interested. Have a big rapport.

It's all about asking the right question to help your client see the problems they may face in the future. It'll be slightly uncomfortable for you, but this is proof it's working."

"That's excellent, Vicky, real respect to you. If only the acoustic shut off switch Salesman had asked the right away based questions, the Gulf of Mexico might have been a cleaner place today. My turn."

So I told her about yes tags.

"Excellent Doug. This is fun; we should do this more often -- sharing ideas, that is."

I could see Vicky blushing a little through the corner of my eye.

"My last tip is the MP3 recording facility on my phone. After each meeting, I audio record all the little details that we don't write down such as Little Jonnie's private school or their upcoming trip to Florida to celebrate their 25th wedding anniversary. That way, I can quickly listen to this just before the next meeting to remind myself of the little personal details."

"First class, Vicky."

We arrived at the entrance to Fanhams Hall in Ware, now a glorious conference centre. The architecture looked 19th Century -- almost Gothic, but I wasn't an expert. The long gravel drive took us to the car parks and then a short walk to reception where we checked in and were pointed to our rooms.

"Thanks for the lift, Doug. I really enjoyed the sharing of ideas. I've also seen that I need to plough into work to get over Nick, so thanks for that, as well. I think there's a course dinner planned at 8pm, I'll see you there."

"See you later Vicky. I enjoyed your company, too."

In my room, I quickly jotted down the things Vicky had shared with me; otherwise, I'd forget.

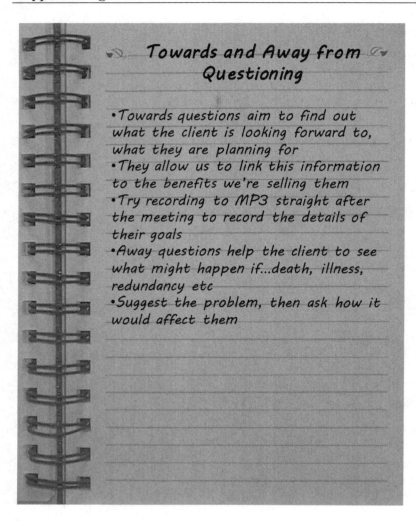

Towards and Away from Questioning

- Towards questions aim to find out what the client is looking forward to, what they are planning for
- They allow us to link this information to the benefits we're selling them
- Try recording to MP3 straight after the meeting to record the details of their goals
- Away questions help the client to see what might happen if...death, illness, redundancy etc
- Suggest the problem, then ask how it would affect them

They had a running track around the grounds and it was only 5pm, so I changed, bolted on my iPhone and running gear. Then I remembered Fred from Taunton and his advice about music and the controller. So I threw the iPhone onto the bed.

Half way through my run, I thought I'd check with the controller.

"Legs, how you feeling?"

"Good thanks."

"Heart, are you OK?"

"Yes thanks."

Hey this was really working

"Ankles, what about you?"

"We're ok thanks, a little pain coming in with the odd track, but we can cope. Keep in touch."

Good old Fred. He was right. I'm just running and not noticing the usual pain or discomfort. I'm gonna thank Fred when I see him on the Forum.

But I didn't need to wait long -- next morning, bright and early for the start of the course.

"Hiya mate, you're not Fred Forde from Taunton are you?"

"Sure am buddy and you're Doug Ballantyne. Hey, did the controller idea work?"

"Yes it really did, thanks, mate,"

"No problem, it's a little known trade secret from Olympic long distance runners."

"So Fred, you're our trainer for the course?"

"Sure am, Doug, I've been running these Package Selling courses for a few months now. I was seconded by head office training as I'd been using the concept really successfully in Taunton branch. In fact, it was myself and David Helms, my sales manager, who developed it."

"What's it like, being a trainer?"

"I love it; quite fancy doing it full time, but the travel here every week is a bit of a drag."

"I'll leave you to it, Fred; you seem to be busy preparing."

"Thanks Doug."

"Oh, Fred, I owe you beer. I'll buy you one later in the bar."

"Thanks, but it'll be just a coke for me. I never drink before a training event and you shouldn't either with the marathon coming up."

I wandered to the back of the room to grab some coffee and started chatting to some of the other guys and resigned myself to give up the beer until the marathon. Jeff's not going to be impressed.

Fred was a great trainer, experienced, knew how to sell, with a sense of humour, too. I quite liked what he did -- might do that myself in a few years' time. But first, I've got to master this job.

Now this was an advanced sales course so I wasn't too sure what this meant, but it soon became apparent when Fred led us down the corridor to the video room. He explained in the introduction that we would recap on the Package Selling methodology, and then we would go into role play with real actors playing the part of customers. We'd be on our own in the video room for a ten minute excerpt that would be relayed to the main training room where everyone would watch. As soon as we finished, it was back to the main room where the group would offer their feedback on how well we did.

Scary stuff, but Fred said he'd start, so that was cool and he also mentioned that previous delegates learned and practiced really effectively.

We were asked to role play three parts of our sales process. The first bit would be setting the scene or what Keith calls – setting out your stall. Part 2 would be a part of the factfind where we would reveal the need for the package of protection. I thought 'the towards and away from' questioning would help there. Part 3 would be presenting the package and getting the customer to agree to the entire package.

Fred went first for all three parts and, boy, was he polished. We drew hats and guess who had to go next? Yep, good old Doug Ballantyne. I heaved myself out of my seat and entered the long mile to the video room. I sat down in the mock office. I had everything I needed -- tablet PC, brochures and all. On the tablet PC I could read:

> In a moment, a Mr. and Mrs. Jonon will be knocking on the door. They've been referred to you by your colleagues in the front office as they've just offered on a property this morning.

The rest of the note gave details of the house, the price and their chain. So I rapidly absorbed the information. The door opened and the red light on the camera lit up. I was off.

Back in the training room I grabbed my learning diary as the feedback came in from the group. I didn't need it as my setting stall, credibility statement was spot on.

A little while later, I was back in the video room for the final presenting of the package.

> "And here it is. It's a mortgage package which will allow you to buy your new home comfortably and if either of you die, the loan is completely repaid and the home is yours. Knowing that your home is secure means you don't have to worry about moving to another part of town and upsetting Elliot and Jenna's schooling. In addition, if either of you are ill or made redundant, we've organised it so that the monthly payments are paid to you for up to one year and after that, if you're still ill, we'll pay you a proportion of your salary until you get better so you don't need to worry about not paying the bills. And the best news is that I've arranged things so that the total monthly payment is just within the budget figure you gave me. What do you think?"

Again my feedback was very warm and enjoyable for me. I seemed to have cracked it. It was the questioning and the self discovery that made it different from normal for me and much more effective.

Fred gave us our evening work, which was to produce a bullet point slide with our main learning points from the group's feedback and we were to present that in the morning.

Later, before joining everyone for dinner, I quickly scribbled my learnings from the feedback and role plays.

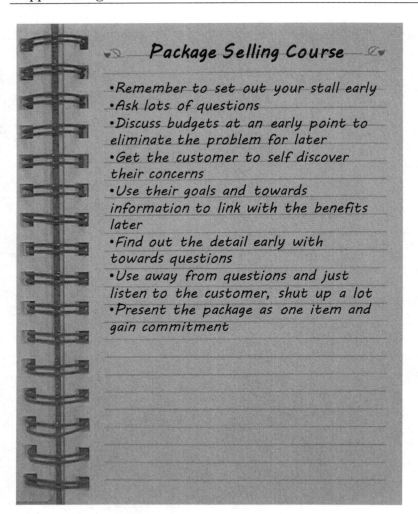

Package Selling Course

- Remember to set out your stall early
- Ask lots of questions
- Discuss budgets at an early point to eliminate the problem for later
- Get the customer to self discover their concerns
- Use their goals and towards information to link with the benefits later
- Find out the detail early with towards questions
- Use away from questions and just listen to the customer, shut up a lot
- Present the package as one item and gain commitment

The course was finishing around 2 o'clock as everyone had long journeys.

I shook Fred's hand. "Thanks Fred. That was a fab course. I really enjoyed it and gained loads of new ideas. And thanks for the copies of the video, I'll watch it later and might even upload it to YouTube. *Not.*"

"Good to meet you, Doug Ballantyne and I'll see you at the Marathon. Keep in touch. Hook up with me on Facebook and LinkedIn. Oh, and by the way, just for the record, your presentation this morning was the best I've seen in a long while. Have you thought about training one day?"

"It had crossed my mind Fred, but I'd better master this first. See you. Have you seen Vicky anywhere? We're travelling together."

"She's over there with Jed from York branch. They seem to be getting on alright," Fred winked.

Vicky was quiet on the way home.

"What's up Vicky? You seem quiet."

"Tired, Doug, just tired. It's been mentally taxing the last few days -- just looking forward to getting home."

I knew she was thinking about Nick, so I put a Kazabian CD on, my favourite band, and sped down the A10 towards London. There was little traffic going into London; most was coming out so we made it to Victoria Station in good time.

"Shall I help you with your bags, Vicky?"

"It's OK Doug, I'm fine from here," as she leaned across and kissed me on the cheek. "Thank you for the lift. I really appreciated it. You're a nice guy, Doug. You'll meet someone soon."

Why did Vicky say that? Is it obvious? Anyway, no time to waste. I'd promised Jeff a frame or two of snooker for 9 o'clock.

"What you having, Doug?"

"Pint, please mate." No, before you ask, a man can only take some advice; some goes beyond the call of duty.

I woke the next morning a little fuzzy. Out into the park for a run before work. Back to my flat, showered, porridge and suit. I was at my desk by 8.30.

I checked my diary. Vince had made two slots for me today -- good man. Vincenzo. And Chloe was due in, as well, to de-brief the training course. The first meeting went really well. I used the stuff from the course and it worked brilliantly. I had the customer really interested in a full package of products – a complete mortgage package as I kept on telling them.

"So how'd it go, Doug?" asked Chloe

"Really good thanks, Chloe. I learned loads and I used it this morning. A really good course."

"Can I sit in your meeting this afternoon?"

"Of course, Chloe and if you can give me some feedback on my package selling that would be great."

After the meeting, Chloe and I popped over to Starbucks for a coffee. It was good to get out of the office sometimes.

"You did really well, Doug -- just more of the same is what you need to do. You've come on in leaps and bounds. Have I ever told you about selling on emotion, not logic?"

"No, do go on."

"Last year, I failed to get to the Glastonbury Festival which I've attended every year for quite some time. Awfully disappointed I was, especially as the festival approached, and the TV and the newspapers were saying what a brilliant Glasto it was going to be and one of my favourite bands – Blur – was going to headline."

"I didn't know you were a Glasto Queen, Chloe?"

"There's a lot you don't know about me, Doug. Anyway to get over the disappointment, I decided to record every piece of Glastonbury that the BBC could show and watch the recordings over and over again as a consolation. The BBC probably shows about 50 hours in total of the festival so using Sky Plus was out of the question since it doesn't have the capacity.

I picked up a new Personal Video Recorder to attach to the TV to ensure I didn't miss one showing of the festival.

I'd cracked it – I could now relax and look forward to watching hour after hour of Glasto, whenever and wherever I liked... Until my husband picked up the gadget and asked what on earth we needed this for as we've got Sky Plus."

"You were in trouble there, Chloe."

"Not quite, Doug. I answered, "Darling, we can use it to do other TV recordings that stay recorded forever and not wiped off by others, we can record movies to watch later, we can use it to store photos when we're on holiday this year when the camera card gets filled up, we can take it to your Mums this Christmas and show lots of photos of us by rigging it up to their TV. I can even use it for work to show delegates videos of their presentation."

"Quick thinking, Chloe."

"It was close. But the point is this. It was a pure logical justification. I had purchased on emotion and justified the expenditure to my husband and myself on logic. So how much emotion do you bring into your sales and coaching meetings?"

"Good question. Lots I guess, but maybe I'll bring in some more. I see what you're saying, Chloe. I need to get into more stories; more emotion and that'll really get the customer buying the package."

"It's a little gift from your sales manager?"

As Chloe said this, I quickly jotted down this little gem in my learning diary.

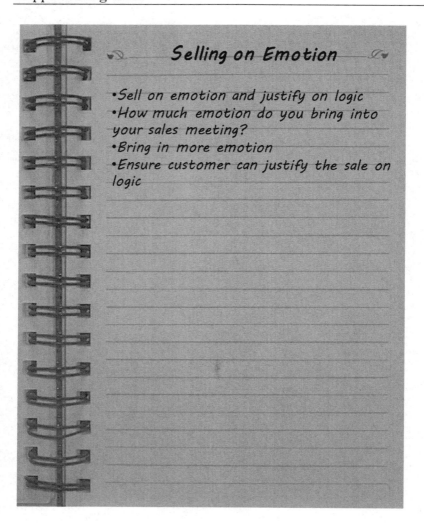

Selling on Emotion

- Sell on emotion and justify on logic
- How much emotion do you bring into your sales meeting?
- Bring in more emotion
- Ensure customer can justify the sale on logic

"Chloe, now that we know each other a little more, what's your secret?"

"What do you mean?"

"You're an excellent sales manager, Chloe, but there's more to you than meets the eye. You seem to give me more attention than the others -- why?"

"No, I share my time equally, honest. Hey, we must get back, calls to make"

A good few days -- nothing's going to stop me now. Wasn't that a hit for Queen in the 1970's? YouTube beckons.

Chapter 9 – I'm sunk if I have another week like that

In which Doug learns to cope with his inner demons that are preventing him from performing

"How long ago was your course, Doug? You know, the one you took that girl from Southampton on?"

"That one in Hertfordshire? That was over a month ago and I know where you're coming from, Jeff. Why hasn't it made any difference?"

"I guess so, Doug. I didn't mean it like that mate, but I thought everything was swinging at work since that course and you were hitting target."

"It was swinging as you put it, but the last couple of weeks have been bad, I mean seriously bad."

And because of that thought, I missed the red in the corner pocket.

"Damn... I can't do anything successfully at the moment. I don't think I'm cut out for this job after all; it just too much pressure."

"Come on mate, what about your marathon preparation? You're doing well there aren't you?"

"Nope, behind there as well. I'm a failure, Jeff"

"Your heads infected, Doug."

And with that, I downed my pint. "At least I can still drink... another pint, mate?"

"What did your mate say again, Doug?"

Chloe was sitting in my meeting room. It was 8.45am, an emergency 1 to 1 called by me -- or rather should I say, texted by me – in exasperation from the snooker room last night.

"Chloe, Doug here. I'm all outta ideas, help."

"Jeff kindly told me that my head's infected."

"Charming friend you have there, but he has a point. I've seen this before. Your mind is beginning to dominate how you feel, maybe your *self* talk is getting you down, Doug. Am I right?"

"I guess so, but what do you mean my *self* talk?"

"What you say to yourself in your head. Do you find that you talk to yourself?"

"All the time."

"That's it, then. Your Inner Game's not working for you."

"First its Jeff, now it's you, Chloe. Both of you are saying my head's infected or my Inner Game is not working. Give me a pill, please."

"I can't give you a pill, but I've got a cracking new business idea that might help you pick up some new business."

"I'm all ears."

"Do you ask your clients for a referral?"

"I always mean to, but I guess I put it off... in case they refuse to help, and it all gets a little embarrassing."

"I thought so. Again, quite common. Let me give you a couple of ideas."

"Excellent."

"Asking for referrals at the end of the process is just too late. Many advisers do it, but ask very apologetically and never sound confident. What I suggest is that you ask for referrals right at the beginning, kind of sowing the seed."

"That seems odd to ask at the beginning. S surely you haven't earned the right to ask."

"You're right, Doug, but sowing the seed is what you need to do -- not actually ask. You tell the customer that you like to grow your business and get new clients in one really important way. You like to give them really good service and if the service is that good, you like to ask them if they know of anyone who might also benefit from what you do. Tell them that once you've given them a great service, and that's what you're going to focus on right now, you'll ask them for referrals."

"I like it. You're preparing them and making it easier."

"That's right. You see, it also makes it easier to ask at the end. Ask them whether the service has met their expectations and recall what value they've gotten from the meetings. When they rattle off the value, ask them who they know who might also benefit in this way and when they give you some names, ask them for the best way to contact. You really want the client to contact the referral before you call, so it's nice and warm."

I chipped in, "What happens if they don't know anyone or they say they'll get back to you?"

"Try asking them again. Ask them if you were to swap jobs, who would be the first 3 people they'd call."

"That's very clever, Chloe. I like that. In fact, I love it. I'll use that the next meeting I have."

I grabbed my learning diary and noted down the points Chloe said whilst she popped out to answer her mobile phone.

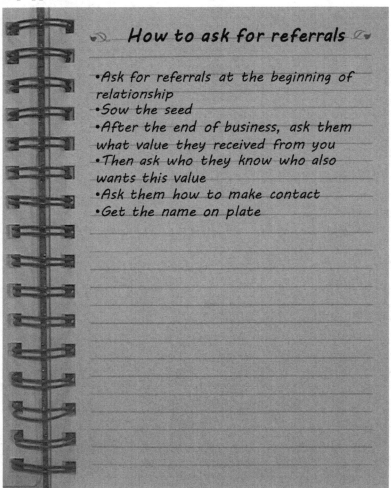

How to ask for referrals

- Ask for referrals at the beginning of relationship
- Sow the seed
- After the end of business, ask them what value they received from you
- Then ask who they know who also wants this value
- Ask them how to make contact
- Get the name on plate

"Sorry about that, Doug. It was James. He's doing a trust evening and has invited me along."

"A trust evening? What's that? It sounds a little bit like tree hugging."

Chloe laughed. She had a pleasant smile, and never seemed to get flustered.

"It does, doesn't it? It was the second thing I wanted to tell you about getting client referrals and I think you should start doing it."

"OK, I'm all ears" grabbing my Learning Diary again.

"James started trust evenings earlier this year. He got the idea from a magazine he reads from the States called Advisor Today. He ran one last month and he bought some nibbles, some wine, glasses, sent out professional invitations that were hand delivered by his clients, booked out the meeting room and put on his best suit. You see Doug, it was trust time and he was preparing to sign the trust forms for his client's protection products."

"Sounds rather elaborate and costly. Keith's not going to sanction the cost of wine and nibbles; he's a challenge to buy a pint in the pub," I joked.

"Yes, . it costs him a few pounds, but it's worth it as he always gets at least one quality referral during the evening."

"Now I'm listening"

"Of course, the forms can be done by your clients who arrange for the witnesses and trustees to sign and return the forms to you. That's much quicker. But if you're looking to replace all other prospecting methods, then you must do trust time."

"So spread the secrets, Chloe, please"

"Prepare the trust time in advance. Get a short presentation together explaining why trustees and witnesses are needed and the benefits to your client. Everyone will be friends or related to the client, so the more you show how well you're looking after them; the easier it will be to impress them. Don't make it a sales pitch – make it a demonstration of your expertise and ability to give tailored advice. Naturally you should ask them for an appointment to review their circumstances."

"Doug, it'll cost the office nothing except some time, and maybe a bottle or two of a good red and a few nuts and crisps. What do you think?"

My Learning Diary was burning hot.

How to ask for referrals

- Ask for referrals at the beginning of relationship
- Sow the seed
- After the end of business, ask them what value they received from you
- Then ask who they know who also wants this value
- Ask them how to make contact
- Get the name on plate
- Sound confident and don't apologise, you give good service

Trust Evenings

- Trusts are essential to protection
- Rather than posting the forms to be completed, invite everyone in to an event
- Invite the trustees and witnesses
- They'll be friends of your clients
- Do a presentation, don't sell, share expertise
- Invite everyone to have their finances reviewed

Chloe left the office and, with a passing remark, said "Doug, you're self sufficient in learning now. Find out how to master your Inner Game, and quickly. Gotta dash.

Lots to think about, but I needed to get on and I promised myself a gym session this evening after work so no trust evening for me.

It was a great session and I felt much more fired up for the marathon which was getting dangerously close. It was after 9pm when I got home so I threw a rice package into the microwave -- these things took 5 minutes to cook and were a really easy meal. I fired up the laptop to read my work emails and my Gmails. Nothing too exciting -- mostly junk, but here's one that caught my attention. The SPA evening talk was on the Inner Game. What a coincidence. Someone up there's looking after me.

The talk title was "Mastering the Inner Game, Resilience Strategies for Pressurised Salespeople"

Brilliant, I need to be there. But hold on, what's the date? Oh no, it was tonight. I missed it. It's not my day, my week, my month. The microwave pinged. Time for tea.

I've seriously got to stop talking to myself.

As I munched on my chicken flavoured rice, I glanced at the email again maybe hoping that the meeting was going to be repeated. No such luck, but it did list the speaker's name. Maybe he has some products on his website I could have a look at and maybe download, just like the Queen and Dane -- or was it Dale or Dean.

I Googled his name and it threw up his LinkedIn profile. No, I should have one of those; mental note to self to set up a LinkedIn page. It threw up a news site about him speaking on a cruise ship in the Mediterranean. Now that's seems like a good life. Ahhh, his blog. Yes, he has a product page. Voila, an MP3 download of his Inner Game speech recorded live at a presentation earlier this year.

Within 15 minutes I'd eaten, downloaded the MP3 file, synced it with my iPod, hit the sofa with a beer and began listening to the Rapportseller....

> "Hi, I'm the Rapportseller and welcome. Tonight I'm going to tell you how to master your Inner Game -- those inner demons, those thoughts that stop you from performing at your best and earning the income you deserve.
>
> Let me start by asking you – are you in famine or feast as a salesperson? Famine and feast can help us determine where we are placed in our Inner Game state of mind. It all depends on how we see things. Do you look out the window and see

constant opportunities, believe totally in your abilities, feel relaxed and focus 100% on your customer's needs rather than yours? If the customer is not a fit and you don't get the sale, so be it; you move on to the next one knowing full well that you have the ability to solve their problems. You don't always have massive sales bubbling, you just know that you will. If so, you're in a feast mentality.

Do you stare out the car window and see scarcity and treat every prospect as a potential customer, thinking that you'd better win the sale at this afternoon's meeting or you're doomed? Are you constantly looking inwards at yourself, some self-doubt? Do you go from one sale to the next, continually wondering where the next piece of business is coming from? Then you're in famine mode.

Of course, we all move from an attitude of feast to famine on a regular basis -- sometimes hourly. But many salespeople I know are in the feast zone much of the time. On the other hand, I know of salespeople that are in famine. Constantly struggling and invariably blaming others for their misfortune. "It's the government's fault" or "the customer was really awkward" or worse still "it's back office support." Customers are never awkward; it's usually us.

The key is to recognise which frame of mind you're in; catch yourself, and then do something to change. It's all how you see things and your state of mind.

Recognise yourself yet?"

I paused the player. I'm in famine right now. I can clearly see that. This is serious stuff; bring it on Rapportseller.

"I think we all have moments of famine thinking and times when we are viewing feast. Sometimes we say "I'm on a roll" which is totally legitimate because you've had some really good results that are spurring on your beliefs and attitude.

Being in feast is different – it's a constant mindset that you have even when your business results are appalling. You just know that as long as you carry on doing what you do, success will come.

Some people say they're on a downward spiral, which is often caused by a series of bad results, dismal luck and events going against us.

Famine thinking again is different. We persistently have the belief that we're not quite good enough, we have to hunt for every piece of business, everyone is a prospect, we hardly ever move out of our comfort zone and are constantly doubting ourselves.

So what's the answer I hear you say?"

Yes please Rapportseller, give me the answer... pleeease.

"Detachment is one answer. Detachment is the secret

I was at the football stadium last month having lunch in a rather pleasant restaurant. It was brand spanking new and the food, décor and surroundings appeared to be sumptuous. I was looking forward to lunch. Talk about aloof, the waitress might have well been an android. She was so detached to the process of serving myself and my colleagues, I thought she was talking to someone else.

It would have been a more enjoyable experience if she had been more attached to our needs, shown some good communication skills and perhaps a little smile. Maybe that was asking too much.

But I want to make another point, though.

In sales we find ourselves sweeping from detachment to attachment. Our challenge is to remain detached from emotions but attached enough to connect and do the sale. The worst case scenario is to worry too much if customer says "no" – and not to take offence, which many do.

If you put £1,000 of your monthly salary onto the favourite horse on the 3.15 at Kempton Park, then you'd be too attached to the race and would be desperate to win it. The prospect of not paying your mortgage would scare you.

However, if you just found the £1,000 and bet on the same horse, yes, there would be emotions hanging on the race, but if the horse didn't come in, your world wouldn't collapse around you.

The same in sales. We need to detach ourselves from the implications of not getting the deal. If you do this mentally, you feel free from the shackles, the stress, the worry of not achieving the sale and you'll enter a place of feast not famine.

The secret to the feast place, is to detach yourself enough to remove the anxiousness that plagues desperate salespeople.

Don't detach yourself like my waitress friend earlier, but just enough to handle the Inner Game issue. Yes, back off when you feel you've become an irritation, but no Mystery Shopper exercise has ever reported back that staff irritates customers and are too pushy. People who are too pushy are attached and desperate – don't go there.

So to be successful, natural, relaxed and persevere with a close…you must be detached, not aloof. Comfortable and connected but not desperate. Believe in yourself, your role and abilities and have a duty of care to all customers."

Phew, I need to note some of this down.

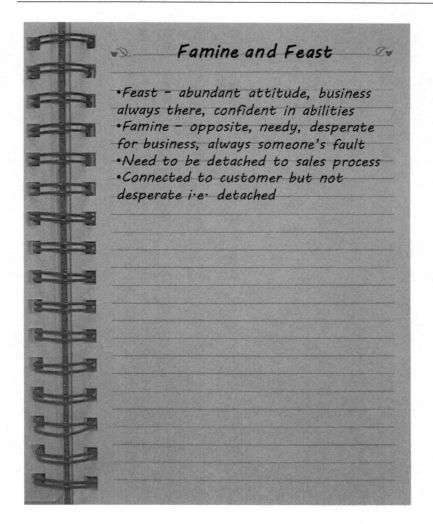

Famine and Feast

- Feast – abundant attitude, business always there, confident in abilities
- Famine – opposite, needy, desperate for business, always someone's fault
- Need to be detached to sales process
- Connected to customer but not desperate i.e. detached

"The other answer to famine thinking is to get your beliefs and attitudes right for selling. So what beliefs and attitudes do top performing feast salespeople have? Here are a few:

> They don't worry about rejection, they just move onto the next client, they're confident of their own abilities, they like themselves, they generally have positive future thoughts, are relaxed, believe in showing up and just performing as always, are open to new ideas.

> They have no need to prove themselves, they believe in solving their customer's problems not just selling them stuff, they're confident of new business, believing that the pie is big enough for all and above all, they believe it's not about me, it's about the customer.

Hey, is that me? Let me jot those down because it should be:

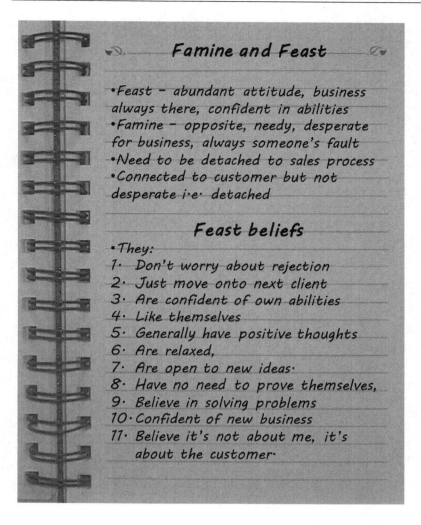

Famine and Feast

- Feast – abundant attitude, business always there, confident in abilities
- Famine – opposite, needy, desperate for business, always someone's fault
- Need to be detached to sales process
- Connected to customer but not desperate i·e· detached

Feast beliefs

- They:
1. Don't worry about rejection
2. Just move onto next client
3. Are confident of own abilities
4. Like themselves
5. Generally have positive thoughts
6. Are relaxed,
7. Are open to new ideas·
8. Have no need to prove themselves,
9. Believe in solving problems
10. Confident of new business
11. Believe it's not about me, it's about the customer·

What about famine salespeople, Rapportseller? Tell me.

"Glad you asked, Doug. They believe in protection first and foremost, think small, have limited goals and stay within their comfort zones, constantly think of themselves and their own needs, don't always like themselves, constantly have to improve themselves as they're never happy with their ability.

They fear the future and worry about up and coming events, fear new ideas and are always asking for approval, asking "Am I doing OK?"

My learning diary was filling with these behaviours. The Rapportseller continued to tell me about famine and feast sales behaviours, as well, and how customers see us in these modes. I wrote them all down.

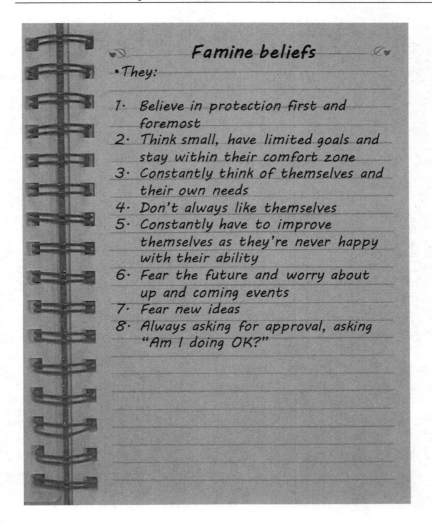

Famine beliefs

• *They:*

1. Believe in protection first and foremost
2. Think small, have limited goals and stay within their comfort zone
3. Constantly think of themselves and their own needs
4. Don't always like themselves
5. Constantly have to improve themselves as they're never happy with their ability
6. Fear the future and worry about up and coming events
7. Fear new ideas
8. Always asking for approval, asking "Am I doing OK?"

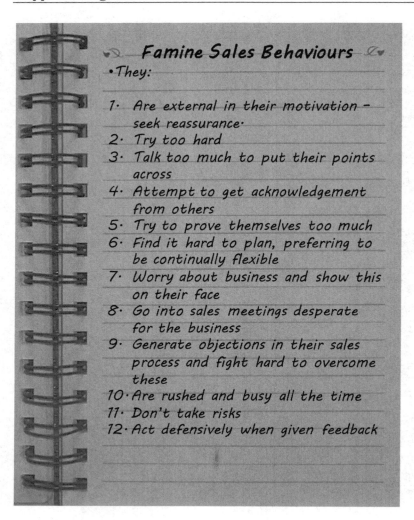

Famine Sales Behaviours

• They:

1. Are external in their motivation — seek reassurance.
2. Try too hard
3. Talk too much to put their points across
4. Attempt to get acknowledgement from others
5. Try to prove themselves too much
6. Find it hard to plan, preferring to be continually flexible
7. Worry about business and show this on their face
8. Go into sales meetings desperate for the business
9. Generate objections in their sales process and fight hard to overcome these
10. Are rushed and busy all the time
11. Don't take risks
12. Act defensively when given feedback

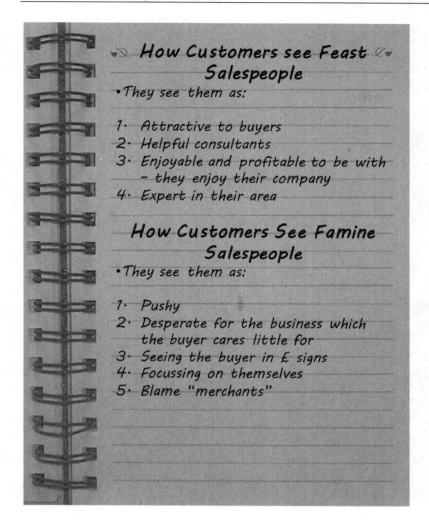

How Customers see Feast Salespeople

• They see them as:

1. Attractive to buyers
2. Helpful consultants
3. Enjoyable and profitable to be with
   – they enjoy their company
4. Expert in their area

How Customers See Famine Salespeople

• They see them as:

1. Pushy
2. Desperate for the business which the buyer cares little for
3. Seeing the buyer in £ signs
4. Focussing on themselves
5. Blame "merchants"

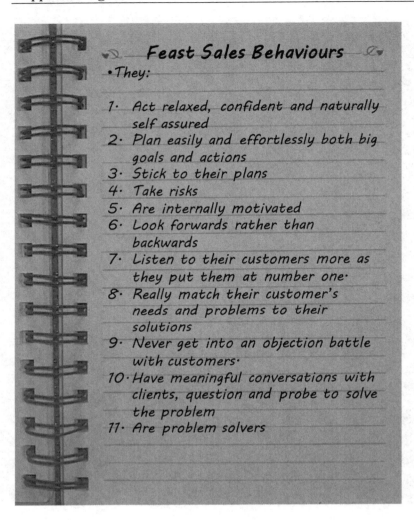

Feast Sales Behaviours
•They:

1. Act relaxed, confident and naturally self assured
2. Plan easily and effortlessly both big goals and actions
3. Stick to their plans
4. Take risks
5. Are internally motivated
6. Look forwards rather than backwards
7. Listen to their customers more as they put them at number one·
8. Really match their customer's needs and problems to their solutions
9. Never get into an objection battle with customers·
10. Have meaningful conversations with clients, question and probe to solve the problem
11. Are problem solvers

I so need to get into a feast style of being. It's not going to be easy, but I can do it. Note to Doug -- stop talking to yourself. OK Rapportseller, what else can you tell me?

> "Next Doug, I'm going to tell you how you can change your beliefs if you ever get caught up in famine mode. It's really easy. First, pick a belief that you want to adopt and make it yours. You might want to become totally confident in your own abilities, not arrogant, mind you -- that stinks. There's a fine line between confidence and arrogance.
>
> Pick confidence and ask yourself the following questions:
>
> 1. What evidence in you supports this belief?
>
> 2. When have you known it to be true?
>
> 3. Who do you know who has this belief?
>
> 4. Why do they believe it?
>
> 5. Do the top salespeople have this belief?
>
> 6. What would happen if you firmly held this belief?
>
> Go on, Doug, ask yourself these questions now."

OK I will. (Is he really speaking to me?) So I noted the questions in the diary and asked myself each one.

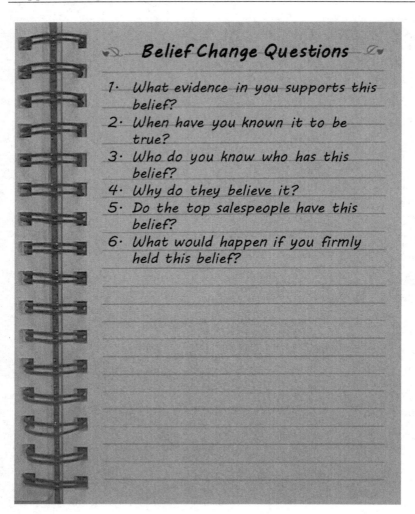

Belief Change Questions

1. What evidence in you supports this belief?
2. When have you known it to be true?
3. Who do you know who has this belief?
4. Why do they believe it?
5. Do the top salespeople have this belief?
6. What would happen if you firmly held this belief?

Let me see... what evidence? Well I'm good at this. Keith says I am, Jeff says I am, I believe in it, too. When has it been true? I've believed in my own abilities before -- after the course last month, in my last job, when I get good feedback from customers. Who else has this belief? Well, Chloe does, Vickie does, Keith sure has -- probably a little too much, but it serves him well. They believe it because they just do. Yes, the top sellers do. I know Fred does and he's a top man in training. If I held this belief, I think it would revolutionise myself and make me more self-confident.

Wow, that was hypnotic. Thanks Rapportseller.

> "That's OK, Doug. Next you want to do some 21-day affirmations. Affirmations are really powerful little tricks that literally re-programme the unconscious mind into believing something else. This is what you want to do. Write down on a piece of paper a short positive instruction such as I am... or I will...or I always... Then repeat the affirmation several times a day for 21 days. This sounds like a doctor's prescription. After 21 days the mind will be programmed to believe in the affirmation. Some affirmation rules:
>
> - Keep them short and in the present tense – I am, I will.
>
> - Make them positive, i.e. to do something -- not to stop something.
>
> - Keep them personal to you.
>
> - Only have 10 maximum at a time.
>
> Try affirmations to embed your feast beliefs. They work."

I will, Rapportseller. Let me jot down the notes about affirmations. I'm going to do some of those before bed.

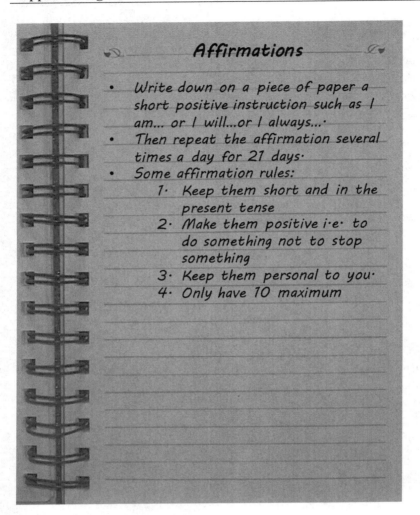

Affirmations

- Write down on a piece of paper a short positive instruction such as I am... or I will...or I always...·
- Then repeat the affirmation several times a day for 21 days·
- Some affirmation rules:
    1. Keep them short and in the present tense
    2. Make them positive i·e· to do something not to stop something
    3. Keep them personal to you·
    4. Only have 10 maximum

"Finally, Doug, I need you to know about anchoring, and no, it's not a nautical term for my purposes today, but a naturally occurring reminder of a state of mind.

One of the most famous anchors known to the travel industry is the sick bag. Just the sight of one of these is enough to turn a level headed and contained stomach wrenching with pain and discomfort. So much so, that cabin crew don't even mention the sick bag anymore for fear of violently ill passengers.

There are naturally occurring anchors all around us. A piece of music that lifts you, your favourite smell, a taste that floods back childhood, a place with happy memories. All these memories or stimuli bring back a state of mind because they take you back to a time when you first heard the music and tasted the food. The state of mind you had then comes flooding back into your insides and arms you with itself.

For example, a favourite tune for me is Oasis and Wonderwall from the *What's the Story Morning Glory* Album. It won the Brits Award for best album from the last 30 years, so I do have decent taste. A favourite place of mine is Blackpool Sands in Devon where I proposed to my wife.

These are all anchors that help us remember what it was like at the time and to re-live the emotions and the state of mind we had. To fire these anchors is easy. For Wonderwall, I play it on my MP3 Player or from my phone and the engagement anchor is simply rubbing my wedding ring.

So how's this useful when selling? A lot.

Here's how it works.

Before you next go into a particular sales meeting, make a mental note of the kind of resource or state you need to perform well. For example, it might be to listen really well, so let's create an anchor.

- Step one – recall a time when you had these emotions or states in abundance. Go on -- think of a time now, Doug

- Step two – whizz back into time and associate yourself with the event. Become the person again in your mind's eye, imagine you are there, once again experiencing the moment.

- Step three – really imagine you're there and re-live the experience – concentrate on what you hear around you... see... feel. Re-live the moment. Now this will allow the state of mind you had at the time to surge through your body, arming you with the resource needed to carry out a brilliant presentation.

- Step Four – is some form of reminder or anchor as we call it. You might want to shortcut to this memory again in the future quickly. Just like a shortcut on your computer or speed-dial on your phone, you need an anchor to help you recall it again. Pressing a knuckle is a touch anchor. You could associate a tune to it or a strong visual – it doesn't matter, you choose.

And hey, presto! You have a way to charge any state of mind that you need at anytime. Really useful for any performer -- particularly salespeople.

Hey, this has been the Rapportseller, that's rapportselling.com. See you all soon. Good night"

The last bit I quickly scribbled:

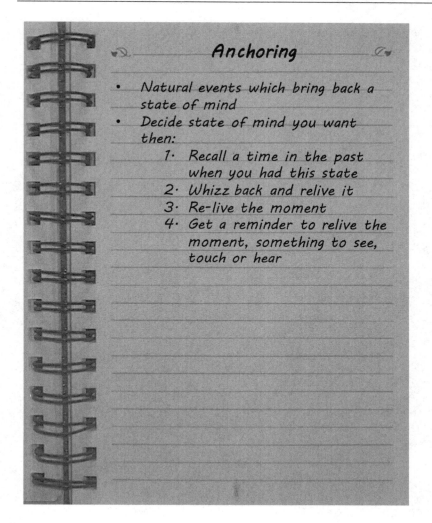

Anchoring

- Natural events which bring back a state of mind
- Decide state of mind you want then:
  1. Recall a time in the past when you had this state
  2. Whizz back and relive it
  3. Re-live the moment
  4. Get a reminder to relive the moment, something to see, touch or hear

I went to bed dreaming of anchors, top salesperson beliefs, famine and feast, and affirmations. The Rapportseller was really hypnotic.

The next morning over my porridge, I wrote out my affirmation cards.

I will believe in my own ability

I like myself

I will have mostly positive thoughts

I am confident that new business will flow

All I needed to do now was to read them every day for the next 21 days and the Rapportseller promised I'd really believe in them. Cool eh? Worth the try.

I must say, I was feeling better and that day my whole attitude had changed. I no longer felt desperate to sell to customers. I felt so much more relaxed, more inclined to listen to customers more, not desperate for the business. Even Keith remarked how I was different.

"Just you don't be too relaxed; we need some deals in this week."

Cheers, Keith, always the motivator.

And sure enough, they came. That afternoon I did a really big deal with a vendor of ours; a great job for them and lots of income for us as well. I think I finally had control over my Inner Game.

The next day, 2 deals -- one from someone who just walked in off the street. Things were going well, so I decided to anchor the feeling, just like the Rapportseller had said. I felt that anchoring to a tune was most appropriate to me, so I scrolled through my iPod playlist to find a suitable track. Here's one and I played it with my ear phones on and anchored that special moment.

The tune? Thunderclap Newman, *Something in the Air*. Try it yourself. It's a special tune now.

As I turned my key into the door, I almost fell over Reg "Hiya Reg, how are you, my friend?"

"Very well, thanks, Doug"

"And Dawn?"

"She's great, too. What about you?"

"Doing well, thanks. Hey Reg, tell me, how do you always remain cheerful and positive?"

"Me? Oh I don't know. I have my ups and downs like everyone else, and my work can bring me down I can assure you."

"Do they teach you anything at the Samaritans on how to keep a positive mental attitude?"

"Yes they do -- let me show you. Do you have a paper and pen?"

I handed Reg my learning diary, and he drew this shape right there in the hallway.

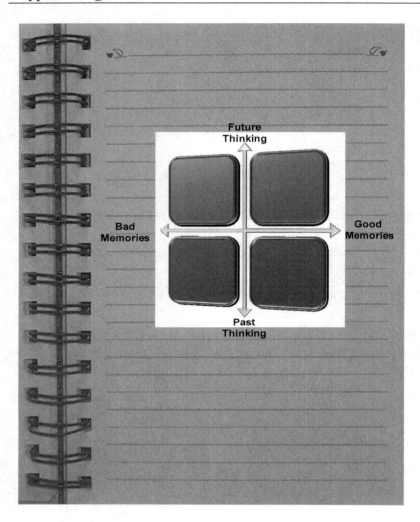

"What does it mean, Reg?"

"Buy me a beer and I'll show you."

"How about tonight, Reg?   I'm free -- just going for a run. Are you free 8.30?"

"Certainly am, young man."

"I'll call for you, Reg."

After my run, I jumped in the shower, dressed, shoved a pizza in the oven, promised myself to eat more healthily soon, checked email, checked Facebook, (not much going on) scoffed my pizza and left to go see Reg.

"Usual, please, Jacob and a pint for my young neighbour,"

"Evening Reg, how're tricks?"

"Good, thanks, Jacob."

"Drinks coming up, Gents. I'll bring them over."

We settled into the snug, a small recess with table and chairs which I thought were a thing of the past, but this was the Kings Head in Stoke Newington High Street.

And Reg began explaining the drawing he so mysteriously created earlier that evening.

"The whole idea of the graphic is to control your inner thinking, your *self* talk. Do you talk to yourself, Doug?"

"Always Reg, always. Do you?"

"Yes and most people do. It's how we communicate with our brain. What we think affects what we do, our actions, so you have to control it and this picture can help you do that.

You'll see that we have four boxes."

Reg grabbed my learning diary and drew a picture.

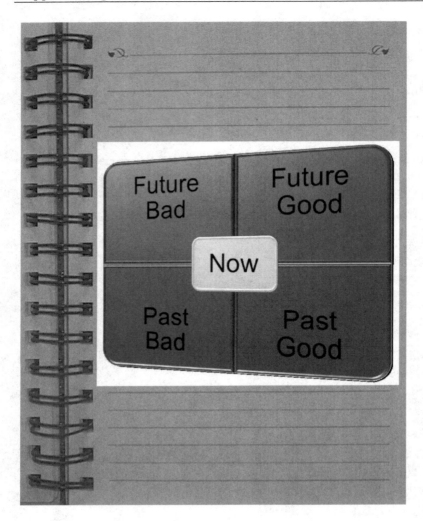

"Each box represents a type of thinking we do every minute of every hour -- past bad thinking, past good thinking, future nasties and future good thoughts.

The plain fact is, if we get thoughts from the past too much, it serves little or no purpose. Yes, some things are useful like nice memories, although these can quickly turn into pining for the good old days. Past bad thinking just hurts. Get your learning and I notice, Doug, you use a learning diary, so well done. Learn from the past error and move on. The past has no place for now. It belongs in the past so just learn to let go of it. That's the key.

Future bad thinking is just as bad, but also useful on occasions. I've got a big speech coming up next week and I've been thinking about this and making sure I'm very prepared and ready, so thinking about it and worrying a little, has helped me prepare thoroughly. However, if I started worrying about it, more to the extent of stressing, that would make things unbearable in my head. Worrying over things you have no control over Doug, has no purpose -- useless, they just pull us down.

Don't claim the stress if you can't do anything about it.

Of course, there's always going to be an element of past bad thinking and future bad thinking, but control it. Don't let it dominate or control you. Spend most of your thinking focussing on now and future good thinking and you'll not go far wrong in developing a positive attitude fuelled by useful thoughts.

Put this picture in your head and focus 95% of your thinking in this area."

Reg drew the picture on a beer mat and told me to hold onto it in my mind.

"Fabulous stuff, Reg. I'm going to visualise that shape in my head."

"What does it say in the middle, Doug?"

"It's your round."

"No, it's yours. Cheers Doug, one for the road."

"Would be rude not to. We both have work tomorrow so must get home, but a quickie won't hurt."

As I turned the key into my flat door, I halted... my body froze. In my head was the top left, which is the future bad. I could see written in this quadrant. Marathon 38 days away.

To put me to sleep, I visualised all the past good things and then the future good things to which I look forward. I hadn't a lot to think about. Maybe I should be populating this. My career, my ambitions, my hobbies, snooker with Jeff, my family... but there was something missing and I couldn't quite pin it down. But by then, I'd fallen asleep.

Chapter 10 – Where next?

In which Doug learns how to plan ahead in his career

I woke abruptly. I had a fearful dream and no, it wasn't Jeff lurching towards me as a zombie. Although that was pretty scary, I'd actually dreamt that I had nothing to look forward to. I'd put every ounce of effort into my career, my job. I think I was there with the current job, business was flowing and I was doing well.

That morning, Chloe said she was nominating me for Adviser of the Year for her area. I was chuffed, and deep down I knew I'd earned it. Adviser of the Year. Wow! Wait till I tell Mum and Dad.

The following evening I ran my first Trust Evening. I'd raided the petty cash tin for some money for wine and nibbles. The condition that Keith put on this, was that he could stay and introduce himself to see if anyone was looking to sell their home. Good for him, as well.

I made 3 appointments with the guests and Keith arranged a viewing for a potential listing.

"Good idea of yours that, Doug. We'll have to do more of them."

So my attention turned to other needs -- the marathon, just 37 days away. I need a jolt of something to really get me through the last hurdle. I decided to hire a personal trainer from the gym for the next month.

Jed was my personal trainer, a really decent guy and he certainly knew his stuff. He was an experienced Iron Man contestant where you run 26 miles, cycle 112 miles and swim 2 and a half miles. He was mega fit, Uber Fit.

On the treadmill, he showed me how to improve my stride and after some practice, it felt so much easier. I was landing on my front foot rather than my heel. We discussed my training plan for the next month; he wrote it down for me and made me commit to it. Boy it was a gruelling plan, but I was determined to do this. I'd too much sponsorship money on the site to let anyone down.

"I want to work with you on something, Doug. Are you up to it?"

"Yep always up to improve, Jed. What do you have in mind?"

"Have you ever watched the Olympic Games on TV, Doug, and noted the sheer concentration of athletes at the top of their game, counting down the moments before their starting gun fires and they enter the most important race of their lives?

Watching really closely, you can see their eyes flicker and move around as though they're experiencing a movie in their head, and indeed, they are.

Ninety-nine percent of Olympians are rehearsing their race mentally, as though they were running the competition of their life or swimming the 100 metres effortlessly and successfully.

Mental Rehearsal has been known for years now to be a valuable way of preparing yourself for a major event. The Soviets used it for years back in the 1970's and we all thought their athletes were using illegal drugs. It's the act of running a motion picture through your mind of the actual event with you achieving great success, before the event has started. This is enough to trick the brain and floods your body with the positive states it needs to win. Apparently the brain finds it hard to distinguish real from imaginary if the *made-up* is vivid enough.

So try imagining a film in your head, with you, the main star, acting out the plot. You're the star of the show. You're also the director -- the Steven Spielberg and you can control the way you act, the resources you have and the success you achieve. Keep the intrigue moving; this is not a photograph, but a wide-screen movie, make it exciting and eventful. After all, it's your imagination. You don't have to tell anyone.

What's your mental rehearsal of the Marathon looking like, Doug?"

"I'm surging through the warm air, full of energy, the crowds cheering me on, I can see the finish line and feel full of power and might, everyone's smiling and I'm smiling inside."

"Fantastic, Doug, really work on that mental movie -- it works."

In the changing room I noted down some of Jed's thoughts.

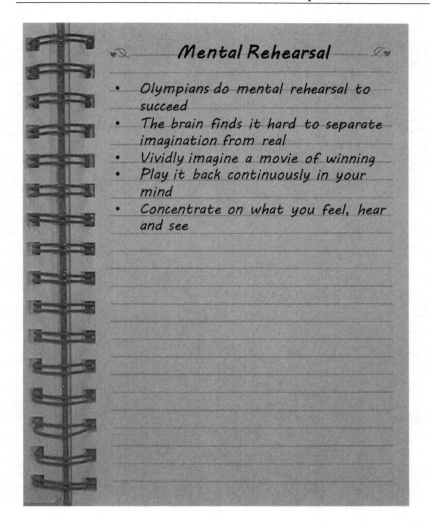

Mental Rehearsal

- Olympians do mental rehearsal to succeed
- The brain finds it hard to separate imagination from real
- Vividly imagine a movie of winning
- Play it back continuously in your mind
- Concentrate on what you feel, hear and see

On the way home, my mobile rang. It was Steve from Chicago; he didn't normally ring so it must be important.

"Hi Bro, how're things? You OK?

"Hi Doug. Yep I'm good. Hey I'm coming over this weekend -- got some time off work. Can I shack up at your place?"

"It'll have to be the sofa Steve, but yea, it'll be great to see you. What's the occasion?"

"Just wanna go see Mum and Dad -- haven't seen them in ages."

"Me too. Hey, we can visit together, I'll fix things up. When are you flying in Steve?"

"Friday night flight arriving Heathrow at 9am."

Sure enough, the plane arrived on time. Steve looked healthy and fresh faced. Although only 2 years' younger, I think he looked substantially younger than me. He'd put on a few pounds, though.

"Hey Bro, see you put a few pounds on Stateside?"

"It's the portions -- they're massive."

We hugged in a man kind of way, finished quickly with two pats on the back and then release. Men learn that technique at a very early age.

Back at my place, we sat on the sofa -- Steve's bed for the next few days -- cracked open some beer cans and shot the breeze. We had a lot of catching up to do. The next day we met Jeff at the pub and then we wheeled into a club until the early hours.

It was a real boy's night out.

We'd agreed to set off to see Mum and Dad on Sunday morning, but we both slept in and didn't get away until gone noon. But the roads were Sunday empty so we flew around the M25, and onto the A3 on the way down to Guildford and the South Coast.

During the journey, I told Steve about Jed and mental rehearsal.

"I've heard of that. In fact, we had some training last week at work on goal setting that uses the same principle. You kept going on last night about wanting something to look forward to. Do you have things in the future, Doug, like goals and things?"

"Yes, I do, but I haven't achieved them yet."

"How alive are they?"

"What do you mean Steve?"

"How alive, how real, how vivid are they in your mind?"

"Pretty much so I guess."

"No, they're not, Bro. I need to explain how you should PACES your goals, that'll bring some life to them."

"OK, we've got about 45 minutes left on the journey."

"So Let's start by seeing what your goals are, Doug."

"Uhhhm… I want to be happy, contented….successful."

"Be more specific."

"In my career, I want to do Fred's job, Chloe's job and her bosses' job."

"Well that's pretty ambitious, Bro. Well done. Which one do you want to start with and I'll PACES it with you."

"Fred's job, a Training Officer with the company.

"Well done, Bro. Now tell me, as if you've achieved the goal, what it's like to have achieved it?"

"Not with you, Steve."

"In other words, imagine you have achieved the goal of becoming a Training Officer with the company. What does it feel like? What can you see around you?"

"OK, I see. I'm at that conference centre, Fanhams Hall. I'm walking into the reception, I'm holding two pilot cases (Fred had two). I'm feeling proud, warm inside, smiling. Around me is the Great Hall, the receptionist recognising me instantly. I have a badge on my suit jacket, Doug Ballantyne, Training Officer."

"Well done, that was pretty vivid. Now is the goal in your control totally?"

"I guess so, it's down to me to achieve it."

"And is it ethical and the right thing to do?"

"Yep."

We whizzed past beautiful Surrey countryside, the A3 was getting a little busy now as day trippers were on the move. Inside the fast moving car, were two brothers totally engrossed in their conversation.

"Now Bro, I want you to work with me on this. Imagine you're moving forward in your life at a rapid pace towards the moment when you've achieved the goal. You know, walking into the Great Hall at Fanhams. I'd like you to head into your future now in your mind's eye."

"OK I can do that. Hey, this is fun. My life is flashing away in front of me."

"Stop when you get to the right point."

"Will do, almost there… stop, I've arrived."

"Now slip down into the picture and put yourself in the story, see the sights, hear the sounds…describe it to me, Doug."

"As I said before, cold day, but warm inside and roaring fire in the corner, pretty receptionist, heavy cases, suit and tie, feeling proud."

" Describe the receptionist?"

"About 5 foot 6 inches, blonde, smiling, cute."

"Next, I want you to slowly come back up and return to now, but this time, do it very very slowly -- taking a mental note of all the steps you're taking to arrive at that point"

"OK, here I go, on my way back now. I'm seeing all sorts of things. Will I remember?"

"Yes, you will, Bro. You'll remember it all because you now know how to achieve the goal. Remind yourself of that moment -- that picture, that fire, that cute girl as often as you can and it will come true. Well done. You did well."

Thanks Steve. What was that process called again? As Steve talked it through, I jotted it down in my learning diary.

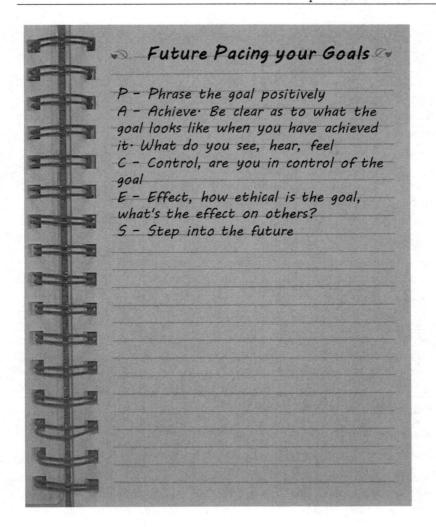

Future Pacing your Goals

P – Phrase the goal positively
A – Achieve. Be clear as to what the goal looks like when you have achieved it. What do you see, hear, feel
C – Control, are you in control of the goal
E – Effect, how ethical is the goal, what's the effect on others?
S – Step into the future

We arrived at our destination, parked the car and walked towards the special place. Dad called over.

"Hi guys. How's your journey?"

"We're good, Dad. How was your journey?"

"Don't be daft," he said through the iPhone screen. "I'm very comfy here in my chair."

Dad was on the phone. We were using iPhone's video programme -- really cool, saved him coming over on the boat. He wasn't getting any younger and travelling in the wheelchair must be a nightmare. We walked over to Mum's plaque at the Crematorium and said *hello*.

Always a tearful moment, but we did promise to see them both and say *hi*. We mustn't leave it so long next time.

Steve's visit was all too quick. At the airport he shouted, "Good luck with the marathon, Doug and that goal you set in the car."

"See you soon, little bro."

The day of the marathon arrived far too quickly. I was incredibly nervous, but did Jed's mental rehearsal the night before, I ran through the entire route, courtesy of Google Street View, in my head and clearly visualised crossing the line.

There were hundreds, if not thousands of people at the starting line, so bumping into Fred was astonishing.

"Hey Fred, how're you?" And we vigorously shook hands.

"Good luck, Doug. See you at the finishing line."

I put in a sprint at the end that I'd mentally rehearsed and crossed the finishing line. I was draped in a foil coat, felt absolutely exhausted but had done it in just under 5 ½ hours so I was pleased... in fact, delighted.

As I wandered away from the competitors towards the crowd, I heard a loud cheer.

"Well done Doug, mate" shouted Jeff. Next to Jeff was Chloe. How lovely... she had come to visit me, as well. Behind her was Louisa and they both cheered. Reg and Dawn were there, too, behind Keith and Vince. What a welcoming.

And behind them all came a familiar feminine voice, "Congratulations Doug. I knew it was in you. Well done."

It was Vicky. She'd come up from Southampton to see me finish. A warm contented feeling spread throughout out my body. I'd done it. Wow. I felt on top of the world.

Christmas Day 2035

I took a sip from my brandy, it felt warm and enticing, the fire was flickering majestically, and everyone was in bed. I relaxed back in my Chesterfield armchair, gazed out into the moonlit sky drenching my garden in its warm glow.

I was looking back in my mind's eye at my life. I still used the positive mental attitude visual that Reg had taught me all those years ago in the Kings Head. Past good, was where I was in my head.

I recalled my success as a financial adviser, promotion to a Training Officer, my first workshop at Fanhams Hall, then Sales Manager, a move to the Southern Region and then finally Sales and Marketing Director. I brought back my personal memories, my engagement, my wedding, my children….all safely tucked up in bed.

On the arm of my armchair lay the present I was waiting to open. It was only something small, my wife had said, something personal. Open it when you have your brandy by the fire and tell me you like it in the morning.

I reached across and picked up the small box, shook it. Nothing. It was about 3 inches by 3 inches, quite light. I flicked the label, picked up my reading glasses and read the handwritten words.

"To my loving husband, all my Love, V."

Chapter 11 – Doug's Learning Diary

In which you get to review everything that Doug has learned over the last few months

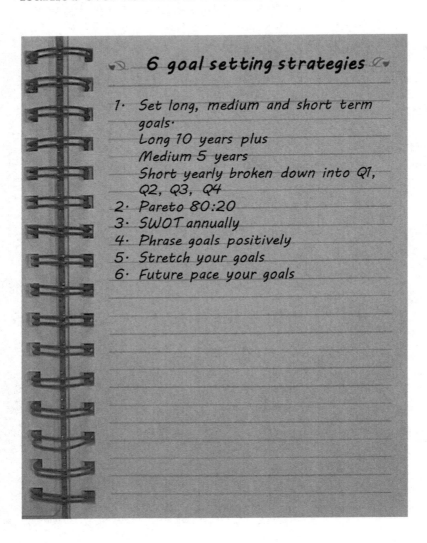

6 goal setting strategies

1. Set long, medium and short term goals.
   Long 10 years plus
   Medium 5 years
   Short yearly broken down into Q1, Q2, Q3, Q4
2. Pareto 80:20
3. SWOT annually
4. Phrase goals positively
5. Stretch your goals
6. Future pace your goals

How to get office based referrals

The key to a referral, wherever it comes from, is for it to be delivered as far as possible, on a plate. Giving some one a phone number to ring, is not a referral.

The team should know what problems and customer challenges my advice can solve so that they can tell the customer about me and how I can solve their problems for them.

Some problems and customer challenges I solve are:

- Time -
- Desire for the best deal
- Right mortgage deal
- Protection
- Trust

Once they've established what situation the customer is in and revealed some potential hiccups or problems they have, then they suggest talking with me as I can help to solve this hiccup or problem.

They are to close the customer by suggesting that they have access to my diary now so can fix up an appointment straight away to see me. My job is to make contact with them to further secure the appointment, but be careful that I don't start selling on the phone. I need to be in mind that I need to secure the appointment first and foremost. After dealing with the customer, I must communicate to the team how I did.

Regularly I need to be telling the team about what I can do, new deals, new products, and new services. My advice plugs the problems and challenges that their customer might have. Make a mental note to do some more training with the team every month as they really enjoyed that.

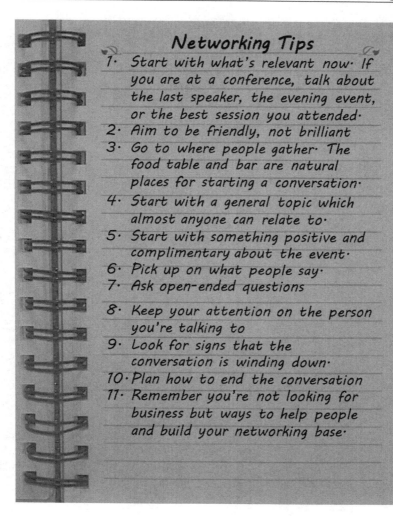

Networking Tips

1. Start with what's relevant now. If you are at a conference, talk about the last speaker, the evening event, or the best session you attended.
2. Aim to be friendly, not brilliant
3. Go to where people gather. The food table and bar are natural places for starting a conversation.
4. Start with a general topic which almost anyone can relate to.
5. Start with something positive and complimentary about the event.
6. Pick up on what people say.
7. Ask open-ended questions
8. Keep your attention on the person you're talking to
9. Look for signs that the conversation is winding down.
10. Plan how to end the conversation
11. Remember you're not looking for business but ways to help people and build your networking base.

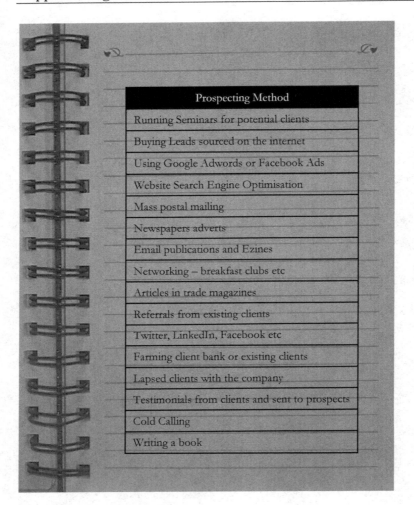

Prospecting Method
Running Seminars for potential clients
Buying Leads sourced on the internet
Using Google Adwords or Facebook Ads
Website Search Engine Optimisation
Mass postal mailing
Newspapers adverts
Email publications and Ezines
Networking – breakfast clubs etc
Articles in trade magazines
Referrals from existing clients
Twitter, LinkedIn, Facebook etc
Farming client bank or existing clients
Lapsed clients with the company
Testimonials from clients and sent to prospects
Cold Calling
Writing a book

Prospecting Method	Value	Headache
Running Seminars for potential clients	9	8
Buying Leads sourced on the internet	9	3
Using Google Adwords or Facebook Ads	6	8
Website Search Engine Optimisation	4	8
Mass postal mailing	7	2
Newspapers adverts	4	8
Email publications and Ezines	7	2
Networking – breakfast clubs etc	8	5
Articles in trade magazines	5	9
Referrals from existing clients	9	1
Twitter, LinkedIn, Facebook etc	2	8
Farming client bank or existing clients	8	2
Lapsed clients with the company	6	2
Testimonials from clients and sent to prospects	8	1
Cold Calling	2	10
Writing a book	9	10

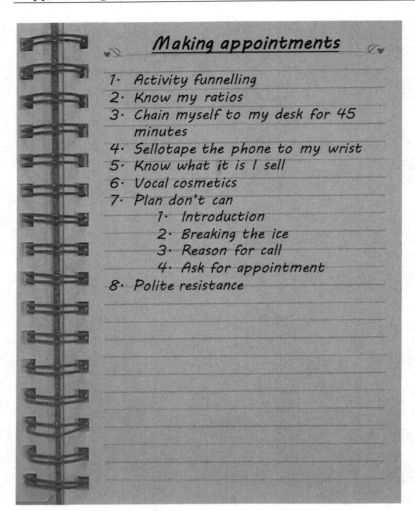

Making appointments

1. Activity funnelling
2. Know my ratios
3. Chain myself to my desk for 45 minutes
4. Sellotape the phone to my wrist
5. Know what it is I sell
6. Vocal cosmetics
7. Plan don't can
   1. Introduction
   2. Breaking the ice
   3. Reason for call
   4. Ask for appointment
8. Polite resistance

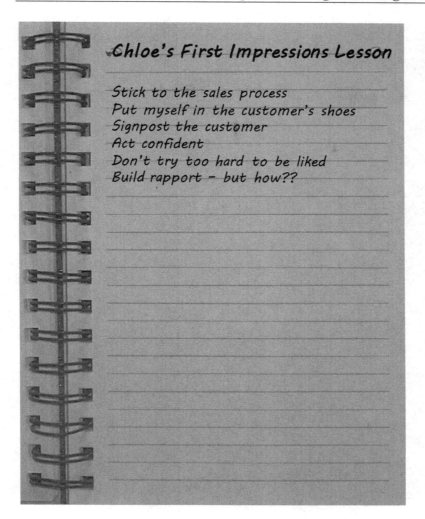

Chloe's First Impressions Lesson

Stick to the sales process
Put myself in the customer's shoes
Signpost the customer
Act confident
Don't try too hard to be liked
Build rapport – but how??

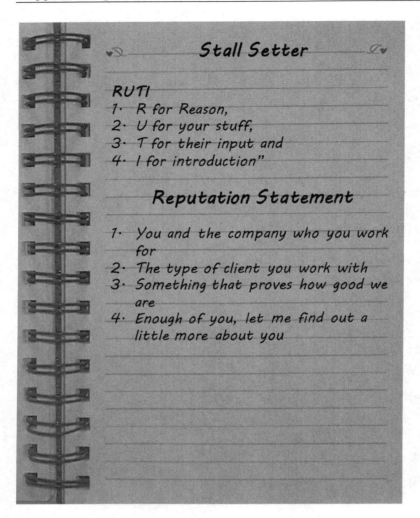

Stall Setter

RUTI
1. R for Reason,
2. U for your stuff,
3. T for their input and
4. I for introduction"

Reputation Statement

1. You and the company who you work for
2. The type of client you work with
3. Something that proves how good we are
4. Enough of you, let me find out a little more about you

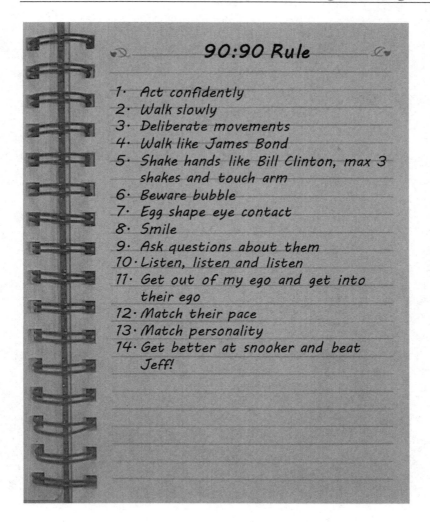

90:90 Rule

1. Act confidently
2. Walk slowly
3. Deliberate movements
4. Walk like James Bond
5. Shake hands like Bill Clinton, max 3 shakes and touch arm
6. Beware bubble
7. Egg shape eye contact
8. Smile
9. Ask questions about them
10. Listen, listen and listen
11. Get out of my ego and get into their ego
12. Match their pace
13. Match personality
14. Get better at snooker and beat Jeff!

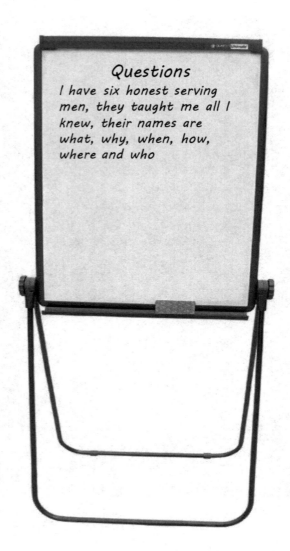

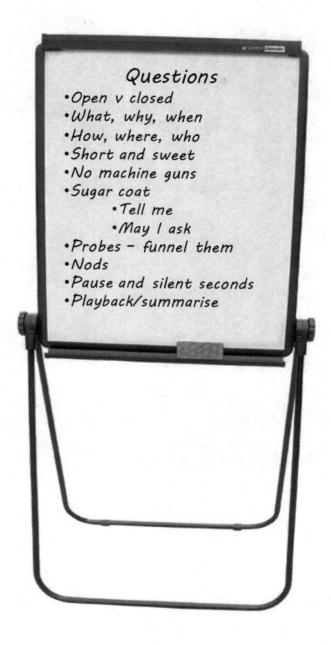

Body Language

1. Combinations of gestures count
2. Congruence
3. Watch for leakage
4. Show positive body language
5. Body Language Model

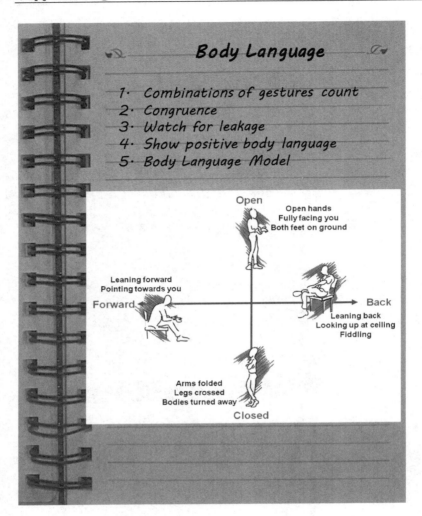

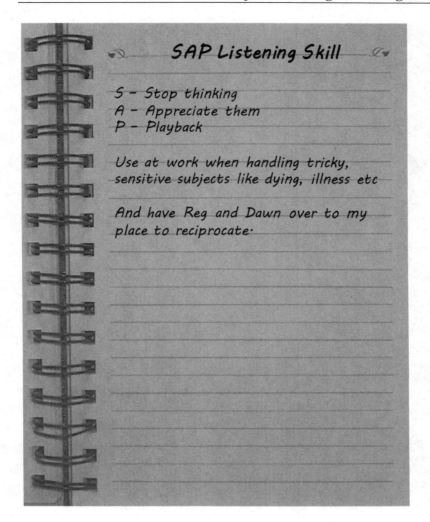

SAP Listening Skill

S – Stop thinking
A – Appreciate them
P – Playback

Use at work when handling tricky,
sensitive subjects like dying, illness etc

And have Reg and Dawn over to my
place to reciprocate.

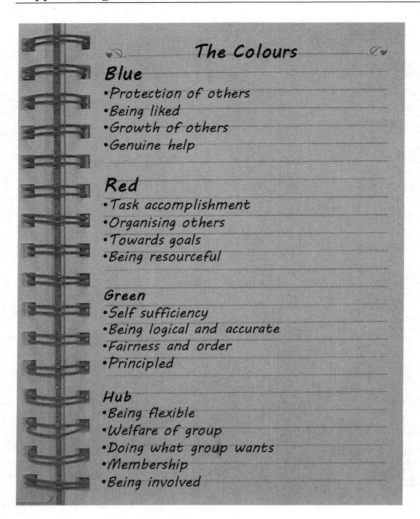

The Colours

Blue
- Protection of others
- Being liked
- Growth of others
- Genuine help

Red
- Task accomplishment
- Organising others
- Towards goals
- Being resourceful

Green
- Self sufficiency
- Being logical and accurate
- Fairness and order
- Principled

Hub
- Being flexible
- Welfare of group
- Doing what group wants
- Membership
- Being involved

How to recognise customer's colours

	Around Them	What They Say	How They Talk	Body Language
Blue	• Photos • People items	• Tells stories, anecdotes • Shares feelings • Informal speech • Expresses opinions • Digresses	• Lots of inflection • More pitch variation • Dramatic • High volume • Fast speech	• Animated expressions • Much hand/body movement • Contact oriented • Closeness • Spontaneous actions
Red	• Awards • Neat Piles • Power symbols • High backed chairs • Minimalism	• Tells more than asks • Talks more than listens • Emphatic statements • Blunt	• Forceful tone • Challenging tone • Loud, fast speech	• Firm handshake • Steady eye contact • Gestures to emphasise • Displays
Green	• Details • Systems • Charts • Organised • Functional	• Fact and task oriented • Limited sharing of feelings • More formal and proper • Focused	• Few pitch variations • Steady, monotone delivery • Slow, soft speech	• Few facial expressions • Non-contact oriented • Few gestures
Hub	• Teams • Membership symbols	• Questions to gather opinions • Inconsistent • Listen more than talks • Compromise language	• Variety of tone and expression • Lots of verbal nods	• Very open • Leaning forward • Non verbal nods • Mirrors body language naturally

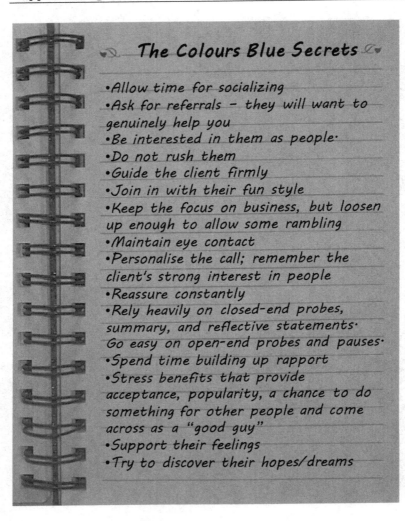

❧ The Colours Blue Secrets ❧

- Allow time for socializing
- Ask for referrals – they will want to genuinely help you
- Be interested in them as people.
- Do not rush them
- Guide the client firmly
- Join in with their fun style
- Keep the focus on business, but loosen up enough to allow some rambling
- Maintain eye contact
- Personalise the call; remember the client's strong interest in people
- Reassure constantly
- Rely heavily on closed-end probes, summary, and reflective statements. Go easy on open-end probes and pauses.
- Spend time building up rapport
- Stress benefits that provide acceptance, popularity, a chance to do something for other people and come across as a "good guy"
- Support their feelings
- Try to discover their hopes/dreams

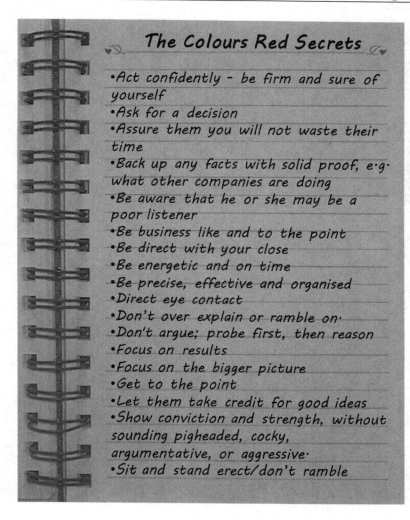

The Colours Red Secrets

- Act confidently – be firm and sure of yourself
- Ask for a decision
- Assure them you will not waste their time
- Back up any facts with solid proof, e·g· what other companies are doing
- Be aware that he or she may be a poor listener
- Be business like and to the point
- Be direct with your close
- Be energetic and on time
- Be precise, effective and organised
- Direct eye contact
- Don't over explain or ramble on·
- Don't argue; probe first, then reason
- Focus on results
- Focus on the bigger picture
- Get to the point
- Let them take credit for good ideas
- Show conviction and strength, without sounding pigheaded, cocky, argumentative, or aggressive·
- Sit and stand erect/don't ramble

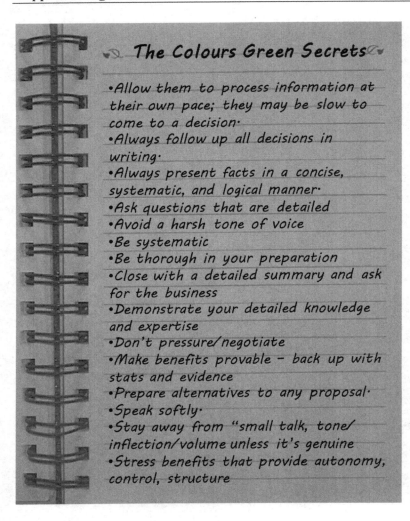

The Colours Green Secrets

- Allow them to process information at their own pace; they may be slow to come to a decision.
- Always follow up all decisions in writing.
- Always present facts in a concise, systematic, and logical manner.
- Ask questions that are detailed
- Avoid a harsh tone of voice
- Be systematic
- Be thorough in your preparation
- Close with a detailed summary and ask for the business
- Demonstrate your detailed knowledge and expertise
- Don't pressure/negotiate
- Make benefits provable – back up with stats and evidence
- Prepare alternatives to any proposal.
- Speak softly.
- Stay away from "small talk, tone/inflection/volume unless it's genuine
- Stress benefits that provide autonomy, control, structure

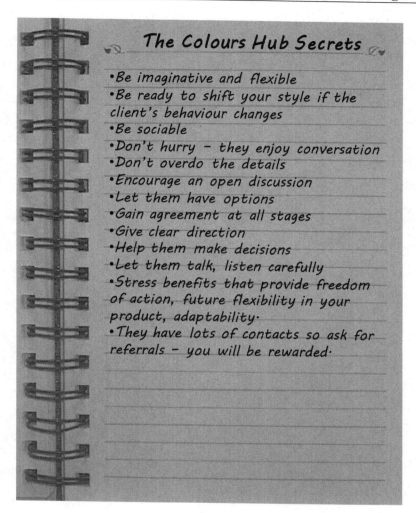

The Colours Hub Secrets

- Be imaginative and flexible
- Be ready to shift your style if the client's behaviour changes
- Be sociable
- Don't hurry – they enjoy conversation
- Don't overdo the details
- Encourage an open discussion
- Let them have options
- Gain agreement at all stages
- Give clear direction
- Help them make decisions
- Let them talk, listen carefully
- Stress benefits that provide freedom of action, future flexibility in your product, adaptability.
- They have lots of contacts so ask for referrals – you will be rewarded.

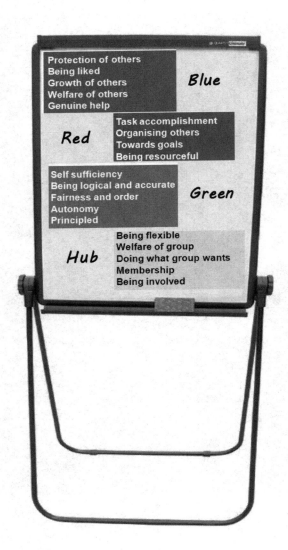

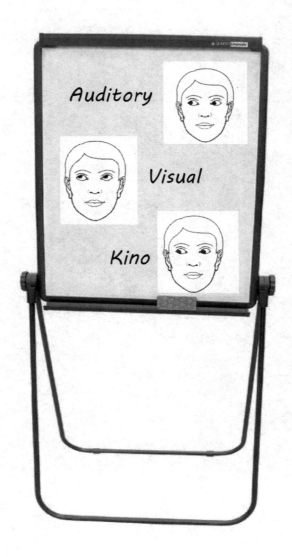

Package Selling

- Step 1 – set out your stall so customer knows you do personal packages
- Step 2 – get to know their situation and problems
- Step 3 – 2fer1 – presenting the whole package
- Making visible what's invisible

Chloe's Presentation Script

So Mr and Mrs Brown I'm really pleased with what we've come up with for you. I've been researching all morning and liaising with colleagues, partners and systems to create a personalised mortgage package that, I think, fits you like a glove." She repeated, "This personalised plan ensures you can buy the home you have in mind with a mortgage that's fixed for 5 years so you never need to worry about rates going sky high and not being able to afford the loan.

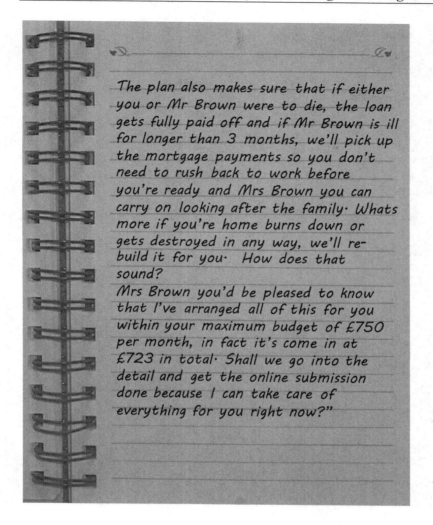

The plan also makes sure that if either you or Mr Brown were to die, the loan gets fully paid off and if Mr Brown is ill for longer than 3 months, we'll pick up the mortgage payments so you don't need to rush back to work before you're ready and Mrs Brown you can carry on looking after the family. Whats more if you're home burns down or gets destroyed in any way, we'll re-build it for you. How does that sound?

Mrs Brown you'd be pleased to know that I've arranged all of this for you within your maximum budget of £750 per month, in fact it's come in at £723 in total. Shall we go into the detail and get the online submission done because I can take care of everything for you right now?"

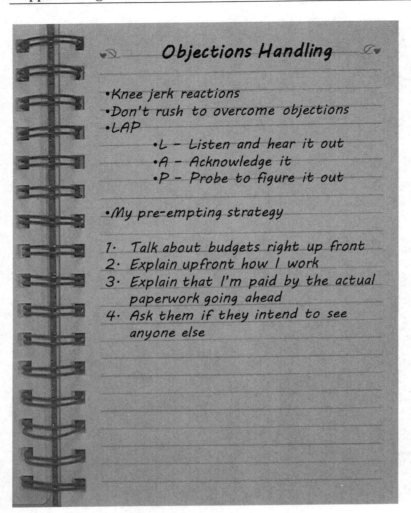

Objections Handling

- Knee jerk reactions
- Don't rush to overcome objections
- LAP
  - L – Listen and hear it out
  - A – Acknowledge it
  - P – Probe to figure it out

- My pre-empting strategy

1. Talk about budgets right up front
2. Explain upfront how I work
3. Explain that I'm paid by the actual paperwork going ahead
4. Ask them if they intend to see anyone else

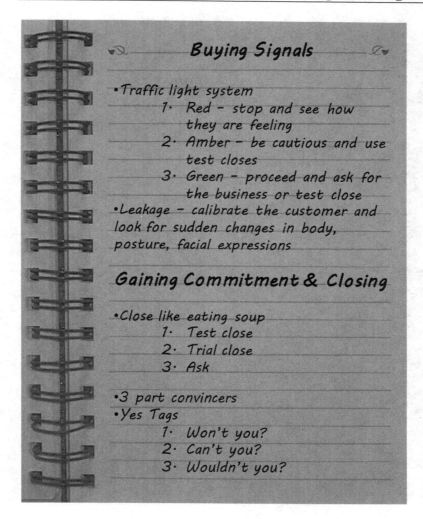

Buying Signals

- Traffic light system
    1. Red – stop and see how they are feeling
    2. Amber – be cautious and use test closes
    3. Green – proceed and ask for the business or test close
- Leakage – calibrate the customer and look for sudden changes in body, posture, facial expressions

Gaining Commitment & Closing

- Close like eating soup
    1. Test close
    2. Trial close
    3. Ask

- 3 part convincers
- Yes Tags
    1. Won't you?
    2. Can't you?
    3. Wouldn't you?

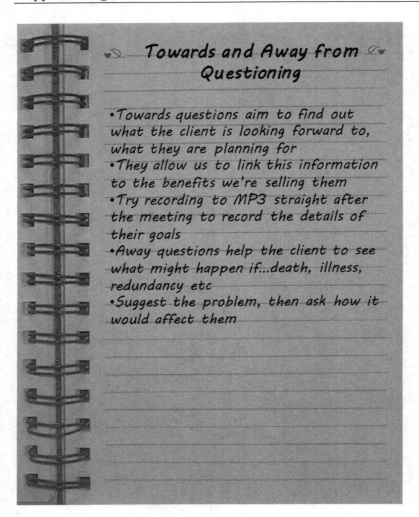

Towards and Away from Questioning

- Towards questions aim to find out what the client is looking forward to, what they are planning for
- They allow us to link this information to the benefits we're selling them
- Try recording to MP3 straight after the meeting to record the details of their goals
- Away questions help the client to see what might happen if...death, illness, redundancy etc
- Suggest the problem, then ask how it would affect them

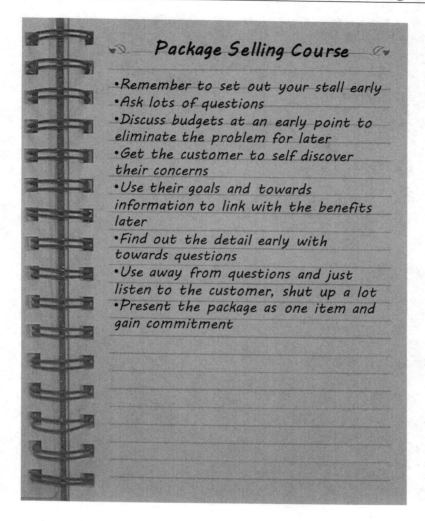

Package Selling Course

- Remember to set out your stall early
- Ask lots of questions
- Discuss budgets at an early point to eliminate the problem for later
- Get the customer to self discover their concerns
- Use their goals and towards information to link with the benefits later
- Find out the detail early with towards questions
- Use away from questions and just listen to the customer, shut up a lot
- Present the package as one item and gain commitment

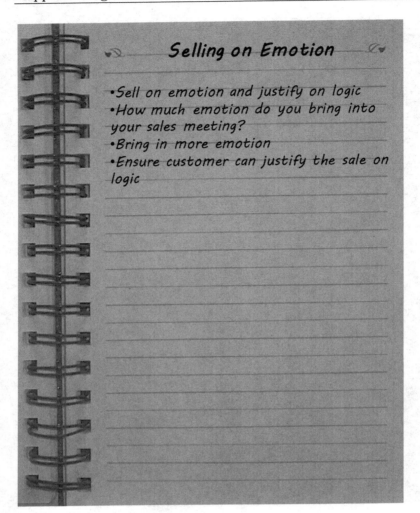

Selling on Emotion

- Sell on emotion and justify on logic
- How much emotion do you bring into your sales meeting?
- Bring in more emotion
- Ensure customer can justify the sale on logic

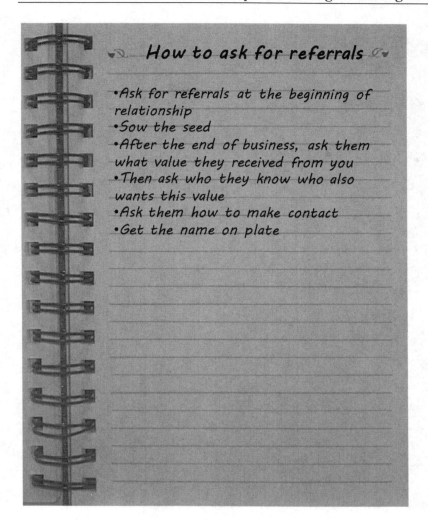

How to ask for referrals

- Ask for referrals at the beginning of relationship
- Sow the seed
- After the end of business, ask them what value they received from you
- Then ask who they know who also wants this value
- Ask them how to make contact
- Get the name on plate

How to ask for referrals

• Ask for referrals at the beginning of relationship
• Sow the seed
• After the end of business, ask them what value they received from you
• Then ask who they know who also wants this value
• Ask them how to make contact
• Get the name on plate
• Sound confident and don't apologise, you give good service

Trust Evenings

• Trusts are essential to protection
• Rather than posting the forms to be completed, invite everyone in to an event
• Invite the trustees and witnesses
• They'll be friends of your clients
• Do a presentation, don't sell, share expertise
• Invite everyone to have their finances reviewed

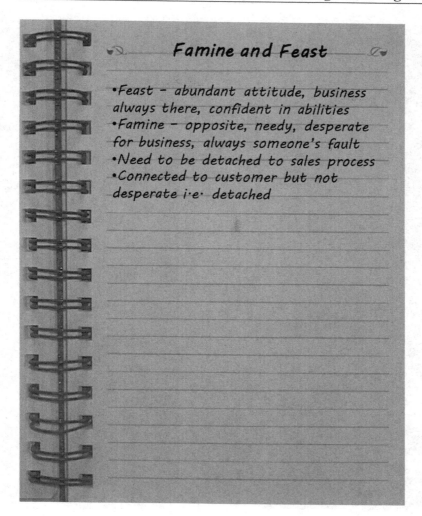

Famine and Feast

- Feast – abundant attitude, business always there, confident in abilities
- Famine – opposite, needy, desperate for business, always someone's fault
- Need to be detached to sales process
- Connected to customer but not desperate i.e. detached

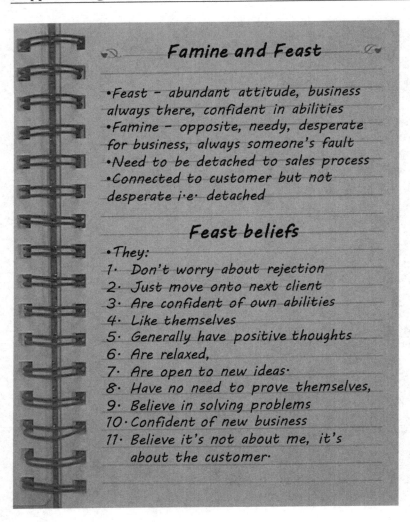

Famine and Feast

- Feast – abundant attitude, business always there, confident in abilities
- Famine – opposite, needy, desperate for business, always someone's fault
- Need to be detached to sales process
- Connected to customer but not desperate i·e· detached

Feast beliefs

- They:
1. Don't worry about rejection
2. Just move onto next client
3. Are confident of own abilities
4. Like themselves
5. Generally have positive thoughts
6. Are relaxed,
7. Are open to new ideas·
8. Have no need to prove themselves,
9. Believe in solving problems
10. Confident of new business
11. Believe it's not about me, it's about the customer·

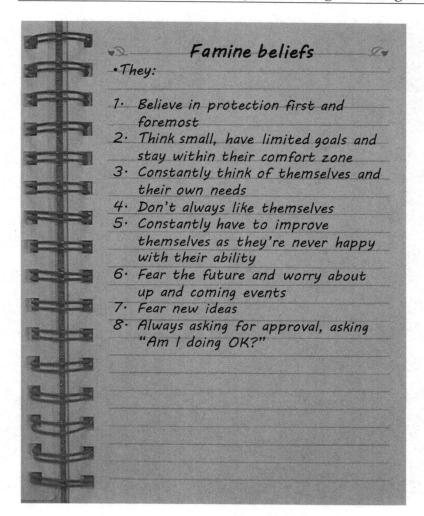

Famine beliefs

•They:

1. Believe in protection first and foremost
2. Think small, have limited goals and stay within their comfort zone
3. Constantly think of themselves and their own needs
4. Don't always like themselves
5. Constantly have to improve themselves as they're never happy with their ability
6. Fear the future and worry about up and coming events
7. Fear new ideas
8. Always asking for approval, asking "Am I doing OK?"

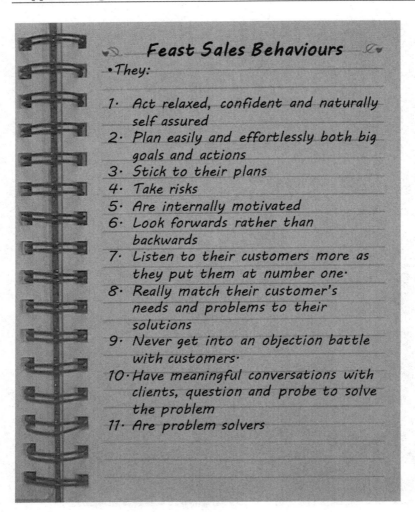

Feast Sales Behaviours

• They:

1. Act relaxed, confident and naturally self assured
2. Plan easily and effortlessly both big goals and actions
3. Stick to their plans
4. Take risks
5. Are internally motivated
6. Look forwards rather than backwards
7. Listen to their customers more as they put them at number one·
8. Really match their customer's needs and problems to their solutions
9. Never get into an objection battle with customers·
10. Have meaningful conversations with clients, question and probe to solve the problem
11. Are problem solvers

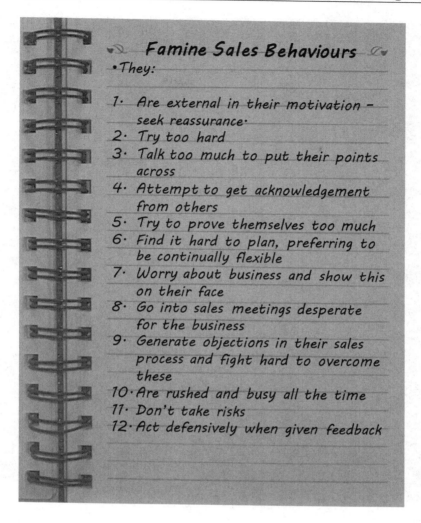

❧ *Famine Sales Behaviours* ❧
• They:

1. Are external in their motivation – seek reassurance.
2. Try too hard
3. Talk too much to put their points across
4. Attempt to get acknowledgement from others
5. Try to prove themselves too much
6. Find it hard to plan, preferring to be continually flexible
7. Worry about business and show this on their face
8. Go into sales meetings desperate for the business
9. Generate objections in their sales process and fight hard to overcome these
10. Are rushed and busy all the time
11. Don't take risks
12. Act defensively when given feedback

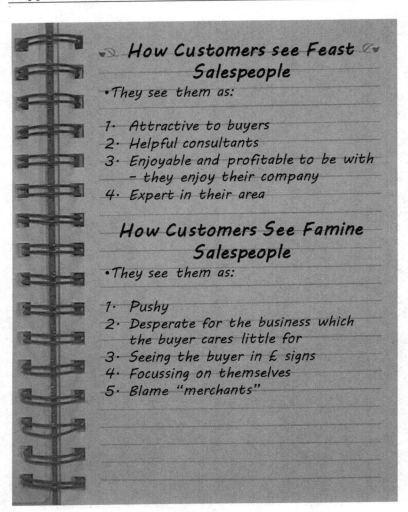

❧ How Customers see Feast ❧
Salespeople

• They see them as:

1. Attractive to buyers
2. Helpful consultants
3. Enjoyable and profitable to be with
   – they enjoy their company
4. Expert in their area

How Customers See Famine
Salespeople

• They see them as:

1. Pushy
2. Desperate for the business which the buyer cares little for
3. Seeing the buyer in £ signs
4. Focussing on themselves
5. Blame "merchants"

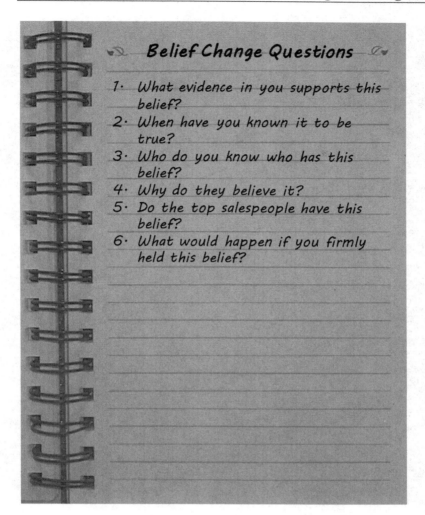

Belief Change Questions

1. What evidence in you supports this belief?
2. When have you known it to be true?
3. Who do you know who has this belief?
4. Why do they believe it?
5. Do the top salespeople have this belief?
6. What would happen if you firmly held this belief?

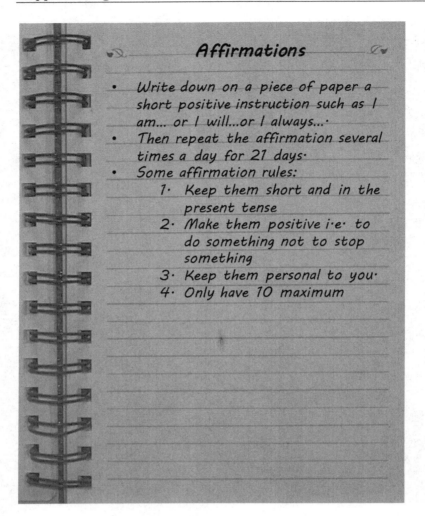

Affirmations

- Write down on a piece of paper a short positive instruction such as I am... or I will...or I always...·
- Then repeat the affirmation several times a day for 21 days·
- Some affirmation rules:
    1· Keep them short and in the present tense
    2· Make them positive i·e· to do something not to stop something
    3· Keep them personal to you·
    4· Only have 10 maximum

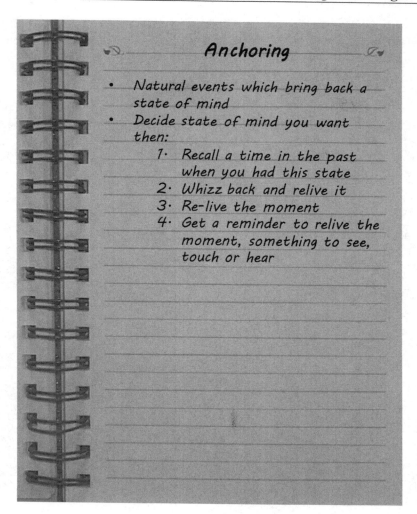

Anchoring

- Natural events which bring back a state of mind
- Decide state of mind you want then:
    1. Recall a time in the past when you had this state
    2. Whizz back and relive it
    3. Re-live the moment
    4. Get a reminder to relive the moment, something to see, touch or hear

I will believe
in my own
ability

I like myself

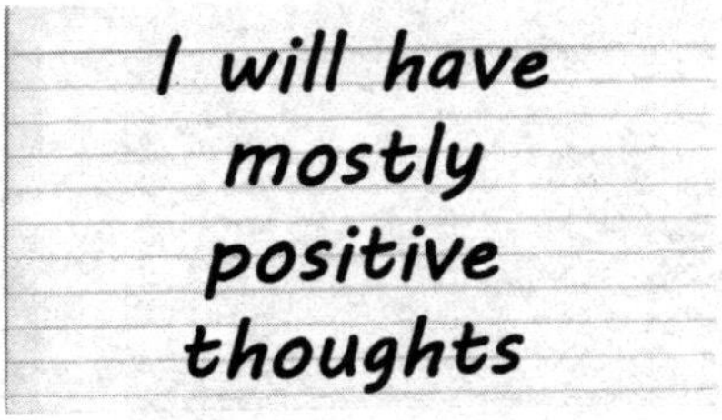

I will have
mostly
positive
thoughts

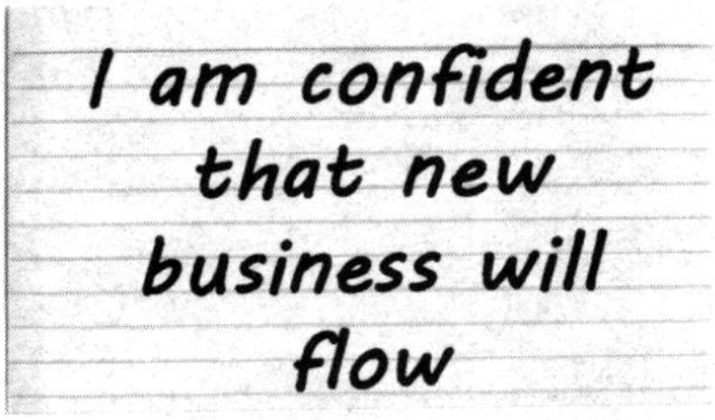

I am confident
that new
business will
flow

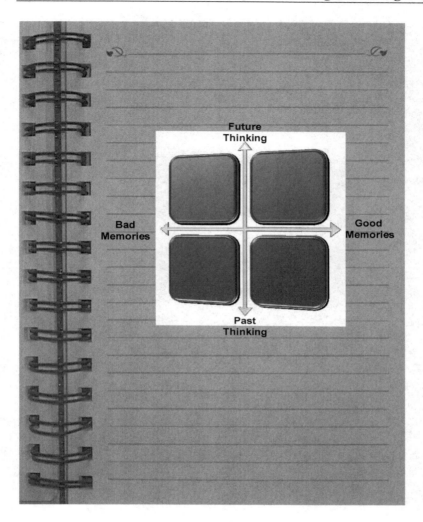

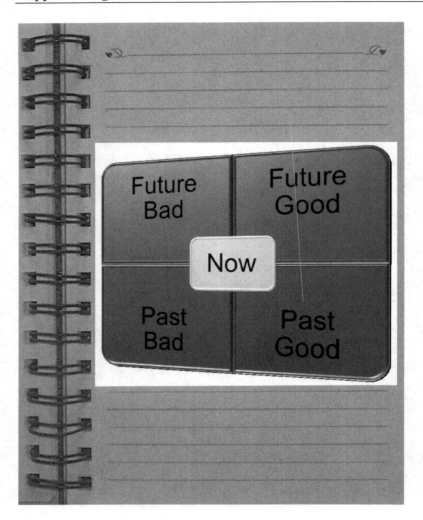

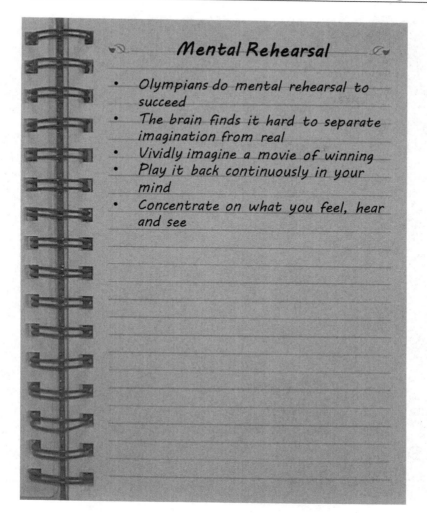

Mental Rehearsal

- Olympians do mental rehearsal to succeed
- The brain finds it hard to separate imagination from real
- Vividly imagine a movie of winning
- Play it back continuously in your mind
- Concentrate on what you feel, hear and see

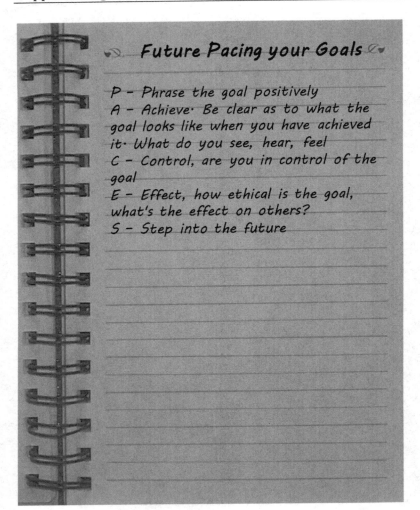

Future Pacing your Goals

P - Phrase the goal positively
A - Achieve. Be clear as to what the goal looks like when you have achieved it. What do you see, hear, feel
C - Control, are you in control of the goal
E - Effect, how ethical is the goal, what's the effect on others?
S - Step into the future